SET SAIL

SET SAIL

MALLARD
PRESS

A QUINTET BOOK

Produced for
MALLARD PRESS
An imprint of BDD Promotional
Book Company, Inc.
666 Fifth Avenue
New York, New York 10103

Mallard Press and its accompanying design and
logo are trademarks of BDD Promotional Book
Company, Inc.

First published in the United States of America in
1990 by the Mallard Press

ISBN 0–792–45354–9

This book was designed and produced by
Quintet Publishing Limited
6 Blundell Street
London N7 9BH

Creative Director: Peter Bridgewater
Art Director: Ian Hunt
Designer: Sara Nunan
Artwork: Danny McBride
Project Editor: Mike Darton
Editor: Belinda Giles

Typeset in Great Britain by
Central Southern Typesetters, Eastbourne
Manufactured in Hong Kong by
Regent Publishing Services Limited
Printed in Hong Kong

The material in this publication previously
appeared in *Practical Sailing, Sailing School* and
Singlehanding.

MALLARD
PRESS

C O N T E N T S

INTRODUCTION

The sailing-boat is an almost perfect invention. It uses the natural forces of wind and sea, creating order and direction from relative chaos. How it does this is a matter of great concern to the sailor: by understanding the theory behind a boat's performance he or she can handle any eventuality on the open water.

The rewards of a good sailor's endeavors are the sense of control attained when the boat performs flawlessly, the perfection of balance between natural forces, and the sheer beauty of the environment in which all this activity takes place.

Sailing is also a high-level sport. At the top end it requires much in the way of equipment – and knowledge of that equipment – to master. Unlike athletics or swimming, both of which rely almost solely on muscular activity and endurance, sailing in addition demands considerable powers of concentration with which to be aware of the wind and the weather, the condition and performance of the boat, the location and activities of other boats, and the dynamics of the water.

Moreover, there are the 'rules of the road' and other precautions necessary for real safety at sea. Navigation is a basic skill that, in theory, is not as difficult as it may turn out to be in practice. Differences between one boat and another may also cause unexpected problems. In all this, however, virtually all difficulties may be overcome through persistence and patience.

Sailing is an enormously satisfying pastime with many facets, from messing about in small boats, to a five-year cruise around-the-world; from the Saturday afternoon club race to a full blown ocean race such as the classic Fastnet.

Sailing has a niche for everyone and barriers are few. You can sail from the cradle to old age just by adapting the type of sailing you do. Nor do you have to be wealthy to enjoy sailing. You can buy a small cruiser new or secondhand for the price of a car in the drive. Larger boats might cost what you would pay for your home, but whereas there are more and more who can afford such craft, there is also an increasing demand for crew.

The fundamentals of sailing remain the same regardless of the size of your intended craft. Whether you are taking those first tentative sailing steps, selecting basic equipment, racing for the first time or embarking on a family cruise, practical guidance is always helpful – if not absolutely essential.

GLOSSARY

A

abaft behind

abeam at right-angles to the center-line

about, going changing direction by crossing the wind bow-first

ahull to lie with no sails set, to drift with sails furled and helm secured

angel weight suspended on anchor cable

apparent wind true wind speed and direction modified by boat's movement

astern behind the boat; moving backwards

athwartships at right-angles to the fore-and-aft line

B

backstay stay supporting the mast from aft

ballast weight used to add stability

bare poles under way with no sails set

batten wood or plastic stiffening in leech

beam maximum width; an object at right-angles to the middle of the boat

bear away to turn away from the wind

bearing the direction of an object from the observer

beat to sail close-hauled

beating sailing against the wind by tacking

belay make a line fast

bend on tie on, fasten

berth place where boat is moored; place to sleep on board

bilge part inside the hull above and around the keel where water collects; curved part of the hull below the waterline

bi-light navigation light showing two functions

binnacle container for the ship's compass

bitter-end the end of the rope which is not made fast

block pulley around which rope or wire runs

bollard short post around which ropes are secured

boom wooden or metal spar controlling mainsail foot

bottlescrew threaded rigging screw

bow forward part of the boat

bower anchor used at the bow

bow roller fitting over which anchor chain runs

bowsprit spar projecting from the bow

broach turn sideways to the wind and waves

broad reach see **reach**

bunt fold of sail resulting from reefing

buoy floating object for mooring or navigation

burgee small masthead flag, pennant

C

cable chain or rope attached to anchor

catamaran twin-hulled vessel

centreboard metal or wooden board lowered through the keel to stop leeway

centreline fore-and-aft line running through the middle axis of the boat

chain plate metal fitting to hold the shrouds

chart navigational map used only at sea

clear air wind unaffected by other yachts or objects

cleat fitting around which rope is secured

clew bottom after corner of sail

close-hauled sailing as close as possible to the wind, as in beating

close reach see **reach**

coaming raised superstructure around the cockpit

cockpit well in deck where helmsman and crew work

companionway access from deck to cabin

compass navigational instrument for determining geographical directions

compass error combined error produced by magnetic forces of deviation and variation

cringle eyelet in corner of a sail

cutter single-masted boat with more than one headsail and with the mast right amidships

D

daggerboard centreboard that does not pivot

dead reckoning process of predicting and fixing position by course, speed, and distance run

deviation compass error produced by magnetic disturbances aboard ship

dinghy small open boat for sailing, rowing, etc.

displacement weight of water equal to the weight of the boat; the boat's weight

douse to drop sails quickly

downhaul control rope to pull down a spar or sail

downwind to leeward; to sail before the wind

draft see **draught**

draught depth of boat from bottom of keel to waterline; amount of camber (curve) in a sail

drogue sea anchor made from rope and cloth to retard drift

E

ease decrease the pressure on a sail

ensign flag showing nationality

eye of the wind true direction of the wind

F

fairlead fitting which guides direction of rope or line

fall off turn away from the direction of the wind

fender soft plastic buoy to protect side of vessel

fetch to reach towards the wind

fix boat's position as established on a chart

flake to lay out rope or chain in a tight zigzag pattern

flood a tide coming in: the opposite of 'ebb'

fluke part of an anchor designed to pierce the sea-bed

foot bottom edge of sail

fore forward

fore-and-aft lengthwise

fore-and-aft rig sails set in a fore-and-aft line: not square-rigged

foremast mast nearest the bow

forestay stay supporting the mast from forward

freeboard height of a yacht from waterline to deck edge

furl tightly roll up a sail

G

gaff spar supporting the top of the mainsail

galley compact kitchen aboard a vessel

genoa large headsail which overlaps the front of the mainsail

gooseneck universal joint between boom and mast

goosewing sailing downwind with mainsail to leeward and headsail to windward

grommet rope or brass ring in a sail or piece of canvas

ground tackle anchor and chain

gudgeon a rudder support

gunwales upper edges of a boat's sides

guy steadying rope for a spar

gybe to tack with the stern of the yacht passing through the wind

H

halyard rope used to hoist and lower a sail

hank fitting used to attach sail luff to a stay

hard chines intersection of straight sides with a flat bottom

hatch covered opening in the deck

hawsepipe pipe for feeding the anchor chain through the foredeck to its locker below

heads toilet facilities

headsail sail forward of the mast attached to the forestay

headway forward movement of a boat

heave-to position used in heavy weather with the jib backed to windward

heel leaning of a vessel to one side due to wind or sea

helm means of steering a boat; wheel or tiller

hike to lean over the high side of a boat when it is heeling

hull the body of a boat

I

inshore sheltered waters close to the coast

J

jackstay wire span attached to the deck, to which safety harnesses can in turn be attached

jib headsail set forward of the mast

jury improvised, temporarily replacing damaged or missing equipment

K

kedge a back-up anchor smaller than the main one

keel fin or fins at the bottom of a boat used to carry ballast and offer lateral resistance against leeway

ketch twin-masted vessel with mizzen mast ahead of rudder post

kicking strap tackle used to control upward pull of the boom; vang

knot one nautical mile (1,852 metres/6,076.115 feet) per hour

L

lanyard short light line for making objects secure

lateen rig with a triangular sail secured to a yard hoisted to a low mast

leeboard board on the side of a boat to prevent its drifting to leeward

leech after edge of a sail

lee helm tendency of a boat to bear away from the wind

lee shore shore on to which the wind is blowing

leeward away from the wind, down wind

leeway sideways slipping of a boat due to wind pressure from the opposite side

life-jacket garment worn to keep a person afloat in water

lifeline line attached to a harness or a boat for safety

LOA length overall

log distance-measuring device; navigator's document of record

LoRaN long-range navigation system based on the measurement of the difference in time of reception of signals from a pair of shore transmitters

lubberline compass mark indicating fore-and-aft

luff front edge of sail; to steer into the wind; to get so close to the wind that the sail flaps

luff foil metal spar around a forestay into which sails are fed

luff groove slot to hold sail in either luff foil or mast

lug fore-and-aft sail with a yard that partly projects forward of the mast

LWL length at the waterline

M

magnetic north direction in which the needle of a magnetic compass points

mainmast principal mast on a boat

mainsail principal sail set on the mast

mainsheet line that controls the main boom

make fast secure a line; tie up

Marconi rig triangular fore-and-aft rig

mark course-marker during a race

mast vertical spar to which the sails and rigging are attached

masthead the top of the mast

masthead rig rig in which jibs are set from the top of the mast

mizzen the after mast or sail in ketch or yawl rig

monohull vessel with one hull

moor to tie up a vessel to a fixed point; to lie to two anchors

multihull vessel with more than one hull (eg catamaran, trimaran)

N

nautical mile 1,852 metres/6,076.115 feet (see also **knot**)

navel pipe see **hawsepipe**

neap tide either of two least tides in a lunar month

O

offshore some distance away from land

off the wind sailing downwind

one-design class of boat constructed to identical design

on the wind beating, close-hauled

outhaul rope used to tension the foot of a sail

overhangs the ends of a boat above the waterline

P

painter line for securing the bow of a dinghy

pilot documentary guide containing navigation and harbour-approach information etc.

pintle metal pin on which the rudder is hung

plot mark the course or position on a chart

point direction on the compass card

pointing boat's heading relative to the wind when beating

point of sailing boat's heading relative to the wind direction

pontoon a floating jetty

port left-hand side of a vessel when looking forward

port tack when a boat sails with the main boom to starboard and the wind hits the port side first

pulpit metal guardrail at the bow

Q

Q-flag yellow rectangular International Code Flag requesting customs clearance

quarter portion of a vessel between beam and stern

R

rake slope away from the vertical either of a mast or of the bows

RDF radio direction finding

reach to sail at more or less right-angles to the wind

broad reach: to sail with the wind abaft the beam and with the sails well out on the quarter

close reach: to sail nearly close-hauled with sheets just eased

reaching sailing on a tack with the wind roughly abeam

reef to reduce the area of sail

reef pendant line used to pull down a reef

regatta series of boat races

rig sails, spars and rigging, and their arrangement

rigging ropes and wire stays of a boat

roach curved section at the leech of a sail

rode anchor cable

rowlocks crutches on the gunwale that hold the oars when in use

rudder vertical metal or wooden plate attached at the stern, whose movements steer the boat

run to sail with the wind aft

running rigging ropes or wires used to set and adjust sails

S

samson post stout post on the foredeck to which mooring lines are attached

sandbar ridge of sand in a river or sea, often exposed at low tide

schooner sailing boat with two or more masts in which the mainmast is behind at least one smaller mast

scope length of rope or chain paid out when anchoring

scull to propel a boat by means of one oar over the stern

sea anchor floating object streamed from the bow to hold a boat to the wind

seacock valve through the hull for taking in water and discharging waste

self-tailer type of winch which grips the rope automatically

shackle metal joining-link with screw-in pin

shank long central arm of an anchor

sheave grooved wheel in a block, around which the rope or wire turns

sheet rope for trimming a sail

shroud(s) fixed rigging to support the mast athwartships

skeg part of hull supporting the leading edge of the rudder

sloop single-masted rig with mainsail and headsail

snatch block single block with a latched opening on one side

snub to pull in a rope so as to bring it briefly under tension

sound to determine the depth of water beneath a vessel; a body of water partly enclosed by an island or offshore bar

spar pole, mast or boom that supports a sail

spinnaker triangular sail set in front of the forestay

spreader strut at the side of the mast to accept compression exerted by the shrouds

spring a warp used to resist fore-and-aft movement of a moored boat

sprit spar projecting diagonally from the mast to extend the fore-and-aft sail

spritsail sail extended or rigged from a sprit

squall sudden storm resulting from extreme thermal conditions

square rig square sails extended by yards set across the boat

stanchion metal post at the deck edge to support guardrails or lifelines

standing rigging fixed shrouds or stays of a boat

starboard right-hand side of a vessel when looking forward

starboard tack when a boat sails with its boom to port and the wind hits the starboard side first

stays wires or ropes used to support the mast longitudinally

staysail sail set on a stay inboard of the forwardmost sail

steerageway the slowest speed at which a boat can operate while still under control

stem the hull at the bow

step piece of wood or metal that holds the heel of the mast

stern the after end of a vessel

sternway backward movement of a boat

storm jib small sail at the bow used in heavy seas

storm trysail small but heavy mainsail used in stormy weather

swinging the compass determining the amount of compass error on all headings

T

tack bottom front corner of a sail; to turn a boat from one side of the wind to the other; diagonal of a zigzag course into the wind

tacking working to windward close-hauled

taffrail guardrail at the stern

tailing pulling on a sheet while the winch is manually operated

tender small dinghy; tending to heel easily

topping lift line from the masthead used to support the boom

transit the lining up of two objects

transom after part of the hull between the waterline and deck level

traveller track for adjusting the position of the mainsheet athwartships

tri-light navigation light

trim to adjust a sail or the flotation of a sailing craft; the way a boat sits in the water

tripping line line to remotely release an anchor or a fitting

true north exact geographical north

true wind wind direction without taking into account the movement of the boat

trysail small storm sail set abaft the mast

turnbuckle threaded screw used to maintain correct tension on standing rigging; bottlescrew

U

uphaul line for hauling up a spar

V

vang tackle used to control upward pull of the boom; kicking strap

variation difference between true and magnetic north

W

warp long rope for mooring a boat

weather helm tendency of a boat to steer into the wind

winch mechanical device for hauling in sheets or halyards

windlass mechanical device for hauling in the anchor chain

windward upwind of the vessel

Y

yard spar used to suspend a square or lateen sail

(LEFT) On a fairly calm day, the balloon-like shape of these colorful spinnakers makes the most of the available wind.

· · · · · · · · · · · · · · · · · C H A P T E R   O N E · · · · · · · · · · · · · · · · ·

TYPES OF SAILING BOAT

It is well known that the early Polynesians used sail power extensively on their dugouts and outriggers and even on their large ocean-voyaging war canoes. Much of the Pacific was settled in these vessels long before the European explorers arrived, and possibly long before anyone in Europe had the technology to wander to see farther than the next inshore bay.

WIND-POWER THROUGH THE AGES

It is also widely known that at about the same time the Polynesians were exploring far and wide, the Chinese were plying the coastal trade routes in Asia in their sea-worthy and able junks. So advanced was the junk as a sailing machine, that the Chinese are believed to have explored as far north as what we now call Alaska. Much later, the British settled in Hong Kong only with the permission of the warlords of China, whose junk fleets were far superior in speed and maneuverability to Her Majesty's men-of-war.

The earliest sailing vessels relied on their sails only for going downwind; they hoisted sail only when the wind was blowing in the direction of their travel. The primitive sailor would hoist his sail in a favorable breeze, square-off before it and get a free ride to his downwind destination. It was certainly better than paddling, and sail power soon became popular. A trader or trapper could load his canoe with grain or pelts and wait for a following wind to sail him and his cargo to market.

But if he wanted to travel upwind, he had to get out the paddle. Obviously this was no trouble when small quantities of goods were being shipped, but when boats got larger, more and more men were needed to paddle or row the extra weight.

Viking ships and Roman galleys sprouted banks of oars and stout crewmen were needed to manage them. Polynesian dugouts carried the whole tribe, paddles foaming in the sea.

Man needed a way to sail upwind, and the Eastern world was far ahead of the West in this, designing workable sailing vessels capable of transoceanic travel – some of which was, of necessity, upwind.

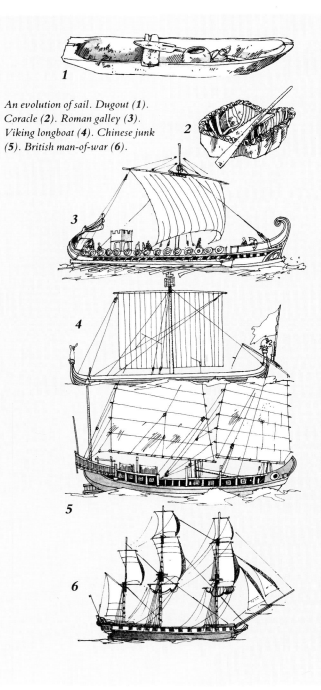

An evolution of sail. Dugout (1). Coracle (2). Roman galley (3). Viking longboat (4). Chinese junk (5). British man-of-war (6).

FORE AND AFT

One only needs to look at the types of early rigs seen in the East and West to see the differences. Western sails hang from horizontal poles or *yards*. These *squaresails* are really most effective when pushed by the wind downwind, and they display a symmetry when rotated around their mast. Eastern sails, by contrast, have *rotational asymmetry*; their area is over-balanced to one side of the vessel's mast. Although they hang from yards, they are shaped so that they present a better aerodynamic surface to the wind on angles other than downwind.

The sails of these Eastern vessels are the forerunners of today's *fore-and-aft* rigs. The Chinese lug rig, or 'junk' rig, had woven fiber sails that were stretched tightly between upper and lower yards, and had many lateral intermediate yards. Lines attached to the main and intermediate yards controlled the shape of the sail. Because the dimensional stability of the junk sail was so good, it could be set at any angle, catching the full force of the wind and using it to drive the ship.

Similarly, the Persian and Egyptian dhow had long asymmetrical yards from which hung its large triangular sails. These sails had no lower or intermediate yards, however, but were *loose-footed* at their lower edges, and controlled by lines attached to the yards and to the lower corner of the sail. Like the Chinese lug, the Persian lug or 'lateen' rig could be angled in the best way to catch the wind.

An ocean cruiser with heavy displacement. Note the full keel and large rudder hung on the transom. The rig is masthead sloop.

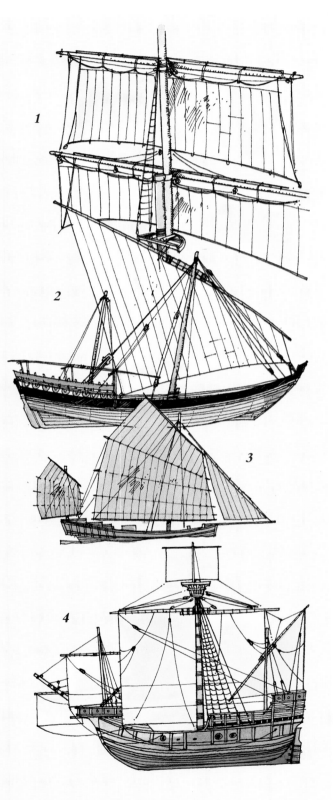

Squaresails were developed in the West while fore-and-aft rigs, like the lateen-rigged dhows, were of Eastern origin; the latter are the precursors of modern rigs.

*Squaresails set on yards (**1**). Lateen rigged dhow from Arabia (**2**). Chinese junk (**3**). Columbus's Santa Maria (**4**).*

Centuries of cross-pollination through trade brought fore-and-aft sail design to the Western world, and it wasn't long before coastal traders and fishermen began using the rig. By the time of the great western explorations, Spanish and Dutch and English ships carried enough fore-and-aft sails on their tail masts to make reasonable headway across the wind and even slightly to windward. Columbus's ships, for example, had lug sails on their rearmost masts, and other derivations forward.

Charles II of England was the first royal to take an interest in yachting as a sport, and it is Charles to whom we owe much of the sport's aristocratic character. Charles, with his brother James, Duke of York, competed against each other, and invited members of the Court to play along with them.

The earliest of these regattas would have been ludicrous, as the boats must have been lumbering beasts of great weight and poor handling characteristics, not to mention poor windward capability. But something in the adventure fascinated the king and his friends, for Charles went on to establish the sport of yachting as it stands today – a sport of competition and camaraderie popular throughout the world.

The yachts of Charles II were heavy, broad, shallow boats derived from Dutch workboats. Because they were shallow, there was little below the water to resist the sideslip to which a boat is prone when under a press of sail in a wind that is perpendicular to its direction of travel. These boats needed deeper *keels* to be able to resist this sideslip.

The Dutch developed heavy, oblong boards attached to the sides of their broad, flat-bottomed coastal workboats to limit this sideslip or *leeway*. These *leeboards* pivoted downward and projected deep into the water, while the breadth of the hulls imparted stability.

Later British yacht designers also learned the value of deep projections below the waterline, but rather than build leeboards attached to fat hulls, they designed underbodies that were themselves quite deep and very narrow. They filled these deep hulls with ballast material (rock, and later poured cement) to counteract the vessel's tendency to blow over.

Both England and America contributed greatly to the development of fore-and-aft rigged sail during the 18th and 19th centuries. The weatherly and swift Bristol Channel pilot cutters of the period bear witness to the level of sophistication of the deep, narrow, heavily ballasted type. A similar look at the Yankee fishing schooner shows how highly developed the shallow, light, broad-beamed workboat had become in America.

Both these types of craft used variants of the *gaff-headed rig*. Gaffs were spars hoisted up the boat's masts on which were laced the principal driving sails of the vessel. These sails were also laced or otherwise *bent* to the masts. At

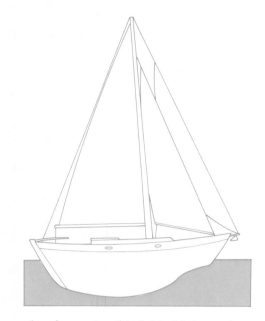

A modern version of the full keel design, with sleeker lines. The rudder is still hung on the aft edge of the keel. This is a cutter rig, as two jibs are set rather than a single, bigger headsail.

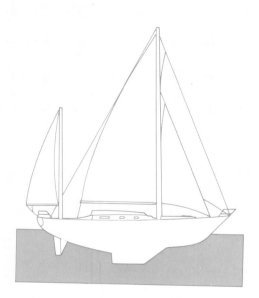

This is the older style ketch rig, with the sail plan split between a large mainsail and a smaller mizzen, mounted aft. The hull has a separate keel and rudder, although there is still lots of volume (displacement) in the underbody.

the mainsail's lower edge or foot was another long spar called the *boom*.

In the gaff rig, the mast provided the leading edge of the mainsail, unlike the lug sail which extended some short distance forward of the mast. The boom and gaff pivoted from the mast to provide the sail's rotation. With the canvas sailcloth of the period, sail shape could be controlled to maximize efficiency.

Forward of the mast were sails similar to those seen on early sailing ships. These tall, triangular sails called *jibs*, were hoisted on fixed hemp lines, called *stays*, and were also designed to catch wind at an efficient angle.

STATE OF THE ART

The last thing eliminated on the way to modern rig design was the gaff. A vestige of the yards of square and lug sails, the gaff served only to create weight aloft and diminish the aerodynamic efficiency of the top of the sail. The next step would be tall, narrow triangular sails.

Designers needed only slightly stronger and lighter materials technology to create the optimum rig. Just a slight leap in materials, and a great leap of faith generated this progress.

The first step was to create rigging strong enough to bear the loads of taller masts. This came in the form of wire cables to replace the tarred hemp of the clipper ship era. With wire, designers could build taller, more complex masts that were thinner in section and therefore lighter as well. *Spreaders* – short perpendicular protrusions from the mast – splayed the cables out and away from the mast, making them even better at support.

Glues were then developed to enable mast builders to fashion tall, thin, lightweight masts that were hollow in section, yet just as strong as the old solid spars.

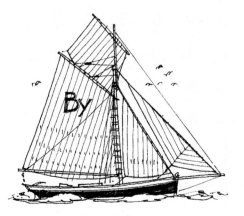

Charles II's pleasure yacht – the forerunner of the sport of yacht racing.

Dutch boeier – an efficient working vessel for shallow waters.

Bristol Channel pilot cutter – a fast and seaworthy working craft.

A J-class racing yacht of the 1930s.

KEEL BOATS AND CRUISERS

A keelboat is a relatively heavy, deep, stoutly-fashioned boat with a fixed, ballasted keel; it represents a type of craft to which many people move up from a dinghy or a small centerboarder. The boat can usually in comparison with a dinghy, carry more crew and may have rudimentary accommodation belowdecks.

She is likely to have what may at first seem complex rigging. She may have two masts, for instance; or she may have a *bowsprit* (a spar that effectively extends the length of the boat forward); or she may have a number of extra sails for use in varying winds; or she may have more sophisticated sail handling and trimming devices.

She is likely to have an engine, with a fuel tank and electrical system and a water system and lavatory facilities (a *head*).

In comparison with a dinghy, she will certainly be heavier and more sluggish to maneuver, yet far more able in a big wind on open water. The ballast in the keel attached by strong bolts or encapsulated into the hull itself, provides stability. The lateral surface below the waterline that a keel comprises also resists sideslip or leeway and helps a boat sail just as a centerboard does.

The combined effects of a keel become obvious when you sail a bigger boat. Because of the extra weight, the momentum of a boat is greater. It takes more effort to stop her, but at the same time maneuvers are slower. Instead of snapping through a tack like a small centerboarder, a keelboat takes much longer, but tends to keep moving through the course change.

There are two general rules to remember in keelboat

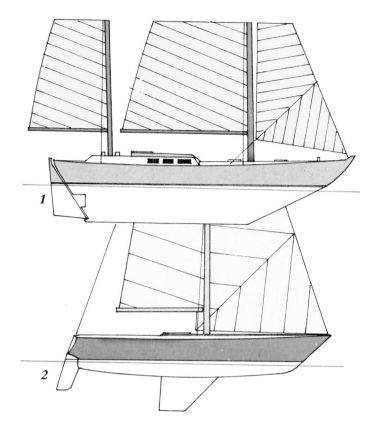

design: (**1**) The amount a boat displaces compared to her overall length will have a direct bearing on her maneuverability. (**2**) The longer a boat's sailing waterline, the higher will be her ultimate top speed.

The first rule simply means that a heavy boat will tend to be more sluggish than a light one of the same

*(ABOVE) Traditional cruising boats (**1**) have long keels which are part of the underbody. Racing yachts (**2**) have separate keels attached to shallow underbodies.*

A half-ton class yacht (LEFT), this is a pure racer.

Finishing a gybe (RIGHT), the crew must re-set the spinnaker as the wind spills from it.

A cruising sloop (LEFT) relies on keel weight rather than crew weight for stability.

A modern lightweight ocean racer (ABOVE) is really no more than a big dinghy, with all considerations of comfort sacrificed for speed.

size. It will develop more momentum (not always a disadvantage) and will be that much harder to turn.

On a heavy-displacement boat, performance is sacrificed to provide steering stability (helped by a rudder mounted directly on the long keel), interior volume, and comfortable motion. Such a boat consequently makes a better cruiser than racer.

A modern racing keelboat's keel tends to be quite deep and quite short. It also can carry much weight in ballast. Combine all that with a very light hull and a rudder separated from the keel itself for improved effect, and you've got a quick, performance-oriented machine with relatively unstable directional qualities but a high degree of resistance to heeling and very effective underwater surfaces designed to resist leeway and produce superior lift and sensitive steering.

The second rule relates to waterline length. There is a hard-and-fast axiom designers use to express the maximum speed a hull is capable of. That speed is called 'hull speed' and is simply the point at which a displacement hull begins to resist any more power applied to make it go faster. It is that point when the boat is 'digging a hole' in the water and will not go any faster.

The formula for determining hull speed is dependent largely on the length of the boat on its waterline: Hull Speed = square root of waterline length (in feet) multiplied by a fixed ratio of between 1.34 and 1.40 depending on the type of hull.

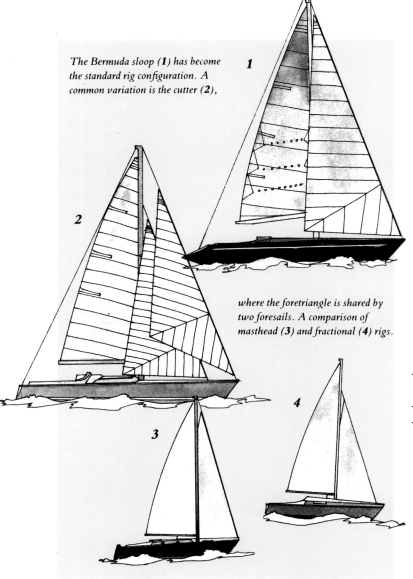

The Bermuda sloop (1) has become the standard rig configuration. A common variation is the cutter (2),

where the foretriangle is shared by two foresails. A comparison of masthead (3) and fractional (4) rigs.

SLOOPS AND CUTTERS

Both sloop and cutter have one mast. The mast could be either aluminum or wood, and would normally be hollow in cross-section. The sloop's mast is stepped (mounted in the boat) at a point slightly forward of amidships. The cutter's mast is normally stepped exactly amidships.

The typical sloop has a *headstay,* a piece of wire standing rigging extending from the masthead (or close to it) right to the *stem head* or extreme head of the boat's bow. The sloop also has a *backstay,* or piece of wire standing rigging from the masthead to the transom. Both these stays support the mast and take rigging loads in a longitudinal (fore/aft) direction.

The sloop also has a set of *shrouds,* port and starboard. These shrouds are pieces of wire standing rigging that support the mast in a transverse (port/starboard) direction. It is common to see a pair of lower shrouds and a

single upper shroud on each side to take rigging loads produced by the boat's few large sails.

The sloop's upper shrouds usually pass over a set of *spreaders,* which are struts attached to the mast port and starboard. The spreaders provide a favorable angle of tension for the upper shrouds.

The modern sloop rig usually has its headstay attached right at the masthead: the reason for the descriptive term, *masthead rig.* However, there are some rigs that have the headstay attachment at a point $^7/_8$ths of the way up the mast, or others that have it $^{13}/_{16}$ths of the way up. These are called *fractional rigs* and are seen on older yachts and increasingly on some state-of-the-art racing boats. To support the masthead on fractional rigs, a set of *jumper stays* passes over small spreader-like struts called *jumper struts* which provide a favorable angle of tension for these short lengths of wire standing rigging.

A sloop has two standard sails, or *working sails*: a mainsail and a jib. Both are triangular. There are other sails that can add flexibility and speed, but the 'main' and the jib are the heart of the rig's function.

There are a number of different sizes and designs of jib. The most basic cut is the *working jib.* The working jib is triangular, and fits more or less within the area described by the sloop's headstay, mast, and foredeck – the boat's *foretriangle.*

Other jibs overlap the mainsail aft and are called *genoas.* A number one genoa laps back almost to the leech of the main; a number two laps about halfway back; and a number three laps only slightly past the mast. Genoas, or 'gennies' all are cut so that the foot runs more or less parallel to the boat's deckline.

Other jibs may also overlap the main, but may not be proper genoas.

There are also *roller-furling* jibs of all descriptions – sails popular on cruising boats because they need not be taken down and bagged. These sails roll up on their own swivel-mounted headstay at the pull of a lanyard led to the cockpit. Because roller-furling rigs are considered inefficient, however, and do not allow the skipper to tailor precisely his rig to prevailing conditions, they are not used by serious racing sailors.

The cutter rig uses all the sails described for the sloop rig, but the cutter has some subtle advantages. Because the cutter's mast is farther aft than the sloop's, her foretriangle is larger, and because the foretriangle is larger, more sail can be put there. The space is more flexible.

Many cutters have a second stay forward of the mast, fastened on deck abaft the stemhead, and run to a point on the mast below the masthead terminus of the boat's headstay (cutters always have masthead headstays). This is the *forestay.*

The forestay can carry another, smaller jib-like sail called a *forestaysail,* or, simply a *staysail.* The staysail can

be used with a small, high-cut jib on a cutter to completely fill a foretriangle yet the sail, being divided, can
easily be handled by a small crew. Instead of taking
down or hoisting one large foresail, two small ones are
there to work with.

A cutter-rigged foretriangle.

MULTIMASTS

Between two and three decades ago, there came a time when boat-buyers seemed to have become quite convinced that for a boat to have two masts implied extra seaworthiness, extra speed or extra power. Designers accordingly concentrated on producing schooners, ketches and yawls.

Actually there is no efficiency gained by adding masts to a boat. In effect, after all, masts are big poles that create disturbances in the smooth flow of air over sails. Nevertheless, there are some sound reasons to explain the fact that a number of sailors – especially cruising enthusiasts – genuinely swear by multi-masted rigs.

On a really large hull, one that must carry an enormous amount of sail to move well, a single mast is impractical, as each sail is so large that it would require a crew of 50 to handle.

Another good reason for dividing sail between two masts is the ease with which sail can be reduced when the wind begins to blow really hard. This is especially true of a ketch rig, where the sail carried by the shorter,

aftermost mast (the *mizzen mast*, which carries the *mizzen*) normally has about the same total area as the sail carried forward of the mainmast, in the foretriangle. So, when the wind begins to howl, you drop the mainsail and carry on in perfect balance under jib and mizzen.

Of all the multi-masted rigs, the ketch remains the most popular. This is probably because of the inherent balance between mizzen and foresails described above. The ketch's sails are also all of modest size, even on a quite large hull, making hoisting and dousing sail easy by a small crew. This makes the ketch especially attractive to the cruising family.

The ketch's mainmast is stepped slightly forward of amidships, more so than a sloop's. The mizzen mast is stepped *forward of the rudder post*, and is approximately two-thirds of the height of the mainmast above the deck.

A yawl resembles a ketch in that there is a mizzen mast. A yawl's mizzen mast, however, is stepped *abaft the boat's rudder post*, and is usually much shorter than the ketch's – measuring up to about one-third the height of the mainmast.

Like many of the multi-masted rigs, complexity – in

This clipper-bowed ketch with bowsprit (LEFT) has an easily managed sail plan divided up into a number of small sails, unlike the sloop configuration.

The most efficient rig is the Bermuda sloop, but the large sail areas require large crews, hence the considerable number of variations (RIGHT) (1) Cutter, (2) Sloop, (3) Ketch, (4) Yawl, (5) Schooner.

The staysail schooner (FAR RIGHT) although less efficient than the sloop, is easier to sail as the sail area is divided into more manageable units.

The opposite of the ketch (almost literally) is the schooner. The schooner rig has its mainmast, the taller of its two, stepped aft – perhaps a third of the way forward from the boat's transom, depending on the design. Stepped at a point well forward of amidships is the *foremast*. The mainmast carries the mainsail; the foremast carries the *foresail*. Forward of the foremast is the boat's foretriangle, which can carry as many as four or five combinations of jib, staysail, *jib topsail, flying jib*, and so on.

The schooner's foretriangle is often extended with the addition of a *bowsprit*. The bowsprit is a spar that extends out over the water forward. It carries at its very tip the boat's headstay, and is tensioned from below with one or more pieces of wire standing rigging called *bobstays*. The bowsprit allows a schooner to set more sail area forward of the foremast, which serves to balance the large sails aft.

These large sails provide the main driving force on a schooner. The mainsail is usually the largest sail aboard. The foresail is somewhat smaller. On the typical schooner, the mainsail is shaped as a triangle, while the foresail is shaped as a rectangle. On older schooner designs, the mainsail may also be rectangular. These rectangular sails have at their top a spar called a *gaff*.

On some schooners, the space between the foremast and mainmast is filled with a number of sails. One sail rides on a stay run from the mainmast's head forward to a position on deck just abaft the foremast. This is the

the form of number of lines to pull on and number of spars to maintain and number of sails to mend and bend and trim – led to the slow decline of the yawl. Its tiny mizzen hardly contributed to the rig's power, and the extra sail only created aerodynamic drag. Finally, when the racing rules were adjusted to account for the yawl's perceived advantages, the rig all but vanished.

staysail. Above that often rides a *fisherman's staysail*, positioned on a halyard, stretched taut between foremast and mainmast, and controlled by two sheets and one downhaul. On this *staysail schooner*, other staysails and fisherman's sails can be positioned between the boat's two masts – so many that the rig is said to be the most complex short of a true square-rigger.

CHAPTER TWO

SAILS AND SAIL TRIM

It is not intended here to overlap with information theory given under **Sail Theory** later in this book. But in order to understand the technicalities of sail trim the reader should have a basic knowledge of the classic points of sail. In summary, there are three basic angles – or points on the compass relative to the wind's apparent direction – on which a boat may sail. These angles are described with specific terms.

POINTS OF SAIL AND SAIL TRIM

The reach When the wind is said to be 'on the beam' and the boat is sailing along a course perpendicular to the wind's apparent direction. Here, the sail is acting rather like a wing, developing lift and spilling the breeze astern to create propulsion. A reach is normally the fastest, most efficient point of sail.

Closehauled When the boat is sailing at an acute angle to the apparent wind, with sails hauled in as far as

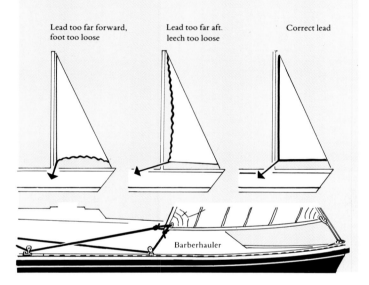

Lead too far forward, foot too loose

Lead too far aft. leech too loose

Correct lead

Barberhauler

Sheet position is critical to headsail shape (TOP). One way of fine-tuning the sheeting angle is to use a barberhauler (ABOVE).

Perfect sail trim is essential if this ocean racer (FAR RIGHT) is to build up a lead at the start of an Admiral's Cup race, but the cruising sailor (LEFT), dinghy in tow, need not be quite so concerned, although he should still seek a measure of performance.

The helmsman watches the telltales on this genoa in light airs (FAR LEFT) trying to keep the boat moving, but he might do better to bear away a little.

An example of high-performance sail trim (RIGHT): running goosewinged downwind with a poled-out jib.

possible. Here the sail is a true wing, developing lift at its leading edge according to the way it is set relative to the wind.

The run Where the wind is astern, and the boat is travelling in the same direction as the wind is moving. Here, the sail is not a wing at all, but rather a 'pocket' which simply catches the wind for propulsion.

Of course, there are points in between:

The close reach The point or points between the reach and close-hauled. The sail acts like a wing on these points.

The broad reach The point or points between the reach

sail is just a pocket to create 'push' for the boat along the wind. Therefore, angle of trim is not as critical. On these points of sail, the sailor must learn to watch his on-board telltales (see below) and gauge the angles at which the wind is striking the sail.

The most important rule is that a sail should be trimmed only so far as to capture the apparent wind.

To windward, the luff of the sail is kept drawing just enough to eliminate the flutter that indicates wind getting around the lee side. On a reach, it's the same thing.

These are basic rules, not designed for extracting the

and the run. Here again, the sail acts most like a 'pocket' in catching the force of the wind.

Achieving the points of sail involves more than simply steering the boat with the tiller. Sail trim is very important, as boat performance depends more on it than anything else.

On a reach, the sail must be trimmed so that just enough wind is captured, and some is allowed to spill away astern. The best way to achieve this trim is to slack the mainsheet away until the sail begins to ripple along its luff. Then trim the sheet until the fluttering is just eliminated. This is called *trimming to the point of draw*, or trimming until the sail just begins to 'draw' the breeze effectively.

On a close reach and when closehauled, the angle of trim will be tighter inboard, but the same principle applies. The sail is a wing.

Note that the reach, close reach, and closehauled (windward) points of sail are those that display the true aerodynamic lift of the modern rig. And it is on these points that effective trimming can mean the difference between sailing poorly or sailing well.

When sailing on a broad reach or run, however, the

absolute maximum out of your rig, but rather for the casual purposes of cruising. Those interested in racing or 'performance cruising' should examine the techniques for more carefully controlling sail shape.

Trimming and turning the rig for maximum efficiency is important both to the cruising passage maker and the racing crew. The latter may be trimming their sails to two decimal places on the speedo. Most crews don't bother to go to such extremes. But remember that a quarter of a knot speed improvement will mean that an 'extra' mile is gained every four hours.

A means of monitoring the sails is fundamental to good trim, so a good number of telltales is necessary on the mainsail and jibs. Telltales are small tufts of wool (or lengths of magnetic recording tape which do not stick to sails) which stream in the air flow. They should be attached to both sides of jibs, about four of them evenly spaced just in from the luff.

On the mainsail, telltales should be attached to the leech by the batten pockets. This is because both sails work in unison as an aerodynamic surface. The golden rule is to trim the front of the jib and the back of the mainsail.

THE SAILS: MAINSAIL

On the conventional Bermudan rig there are two principal sails, the headsail or jib forward of the mast and the mainsail abaft of it. Both are triangular and the corners and edges bear the same names.

Dinghy sailors will be familiar with the terms (see box copy for dinghy methodology). Those who come fresh from dinghy sailing to handling the rigging on a larger boat will find the gear to control the sails more complex. Taking the corners first, the bottom corner at the front is called the tack while that at the back end of the sail is the clew. At the top is the head. In between the tack and the head is the front or leading edge of the sail known as the luff, the trailing edge between head and clew is the leech while the bottom between clew and tack is simply called the foot.

The mainsail and headsail differ in the way they are set. The headsail's or jib's luff is set on the forestay while the mainsail is attached to the mast. The jib's foot is free, while that of the mainsail is attached to the boom. For this reason, there is far greater control over the mainsail than any other sail.

Hoisting the mainsail is quite straightforward. First, find the foot; from it locate the clew and feed it into the gooseneck end of the boom. When the foot is stretched out straight, shackle the tack cringle or eye on to the fitting by the gooseneck and tension the outhaul attached from another eye at the clew to the end of the boom. A small purchase may be fitted for this, or merely a lanyard which is looped through and through.

Returning to the front end of the boom, work along the luff of the mainsail from the tack upwards. This will remove any twists in it. At the head there will be another cringle or more heavily reinforced headboard to which the halyard is attached. Again look out for twists – the halyard may be caught around the shrouds or a spreader end. Then feed the head into the groove on the aft face of the mast. There should be some sort of feeder here – either just a soft-mouthed opening, or if slides are attached to the luff, a 'gate' arrangement.

Before hoisting the mainsail, make sure the battens are in the leech. These help support the mainsail's trailing edge. If they are tapered, ensure the thinner end goes into the belly of the sail and if the battens are of different length, mark which pocket they belong to. Generally, the two small ones go top and bottom with the larger pair in between. A sensible precaution is to lightly stitch over the end of the pocket, to keep the battens from shaking out accidentally.

With the mainsheet (which controls the mainsail) eased, the sail is ready for hoisting. Make sure that the boat is head to wind and that all the sail ties are off. The luff should be tensioned so that it is firm but not stretched. If a topping lift is rigged to the after end of the boom, this can be released after hoisting.

The halyard can be cleated-off and the halyard coiled. Some modern boats now have a rope clutch or jammer for their halyard. If a conventional horn cleat is used, the halyard should be taken around once, then in a figure-of-eight, and either jammed off with another complete

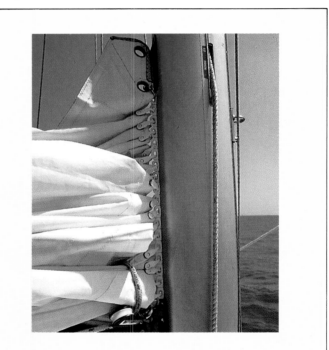

The mainsail is ready for hoisting. The sail is held in the luff groove of the mast by slides.

The boat should be head to wind when the mainsail is hoisted. Take care not to overtension the sail.

loop or a locking hitch. Some sailors disapprove of the latter practice, but if it is done carefully, synthetic halyards can be released under load. Coil the halyard with a twist in each loop to flatten the rope. When there's about 3ft (1m) of rope left, take three turns around the coil and pull the last one through from the back, over the top and hook it on to the top horn of the cleat.

HOISTING THE MAINSAIL IN A DINGHY

Sometimes, the mainsail may be hoisted on the mast before the boom is rigged. But often it is done in this order.

(1) The mainsail, or 'main', is first fitted to the boom, via a set of slides on the sail which attach to a track on the boom; or a groove in the boom might accept the sail's footrope; or the sail may not attach at all along its foot, but simply be stretched along the boom between its tack and its clew. (This last is a type of *loose-footed* mainsail.)

(2) The sail is then attached to the mast via a set of slides on the sail and a mast-mounted track, or a groove on the mast and a corresponding luffrope on the sail.

(3) The outhaul is made fast to the clew of the mainsail, and the tack fitting is secured to the tack of the sail at the gooseneck. The sail is then stretched (not too tightly) along the boom.

(4) The main halyard is attached to the head of the mainsail, and the sail is hoisted. Make sure the slides or luffrope moves smoothly along track or groove while hoisting the sail. The skipper should take care to see that the mainsheet is running free, and the boat is pointed to windward so that the sail will dump all its wind (keeping the boom from swinging away from the boat). The main halyard is belayed firmly at its cleat so that the luff of the sail is in modest tension – enough to take the wrinkles out of the luffrope and adjacent sail panels.

This masthead sloop powering to windward under main and genoa clearly illustrates how the two sails complement each other as foils.

The reefed mainsail is set again (FAR LEFT).

The next reduction of sail area is a smaller jib (LEFT).

HEADSAILS: THE JIB

The jib – or jib and staysail, or yankee and staysail, or staysail and flying jib and jib – is a main driving force in a big boat's rig. On a modern sloop rig, it's fair to say that the jib or genoa provides more drive than the mainsail. Main and jib form one of the most aerodynamic sail designs ever created.

There is no question that headsails help a boat go to windward. They do so by providing a second airfoil, and therefore a 'lifting' surface to help draw the boat forward in the water. In other words, two wings are better than one, but there's something else, too.

During the last century of headsail development, designers discovered an interesting thing. When a headsail was brought into a close relationship with either another headsail or the mainsail, and when the boat was trimmed in such a way that this proximity had both sails set perfectly for a windward beat, there was a perceivable increase in speed, beyond what could normally be expected as the simple sum of the two parts.

Many explanations have been offered for this phenomenon – often called the *slot* effect. Designers agree that it is the result of the overlapping of two or more sails. The overlap – like one formed between a genoa jib and a main, or between two headsails on a cutter – produces a 'slot' through which air redirected off the leading sail is channelled.

Today's naval architects have taken full advantage of this slot principle by building boats with very tall masts

The cruising chute is a cross between a big genoa and a spinnaker.

HOISTING THE HEADSAIL

If the sail has been bagged correctly, the tack will be the first corner to come out of the bag. This is attached either to a special stemhead fitting or with a shackle which is kept captive on the sail or on the fitting itself.

Then the luff must be attached to the forestay. Metal snap shackles or piston hanks are used and, as with the mainsail, work up from the tack to remove twists. Once the sail is secure, the bag can be unclipped from the lifelines and taken below.

Returning to the foredeck, you can collect the halyard from the mast and after looking aloft to make sure it is not fouled, attach it to the head. Finally, the sheets need to be attached, one per side with neat bowlines. Such knots are preferable to shackles, in case a flogging sail accidentally hits the crew. If the sail is not to be hoisted straightaway, secure it to the lifelines with sail ties.

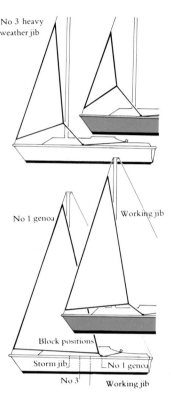

No 3 heavy weather jib

No 1 genoa   Working jib

Block positions

Storm jib   No 1 genoa

No 3   Working jib

JIBS AND BLOCK POSITIONS

The 'gun mount' or fixed spinnaker pole (BELOW) is a novel answer to spinnaker handling, and enables the sail to be controlled at all times.

and short main booms – in other words, tall, narrow sails. These *high aspect-ratio* rigs have more leading edge than other, older rigs – simply by virtue of the length of their headstays and masts. The longer the leading edge on the mainsail, the longer the slot or venturi. They can, therefore, develop much more lift when on a beat, especially when using genoa jibs with 150 per cent or more overlap (or 'number one' genoas) to enlarge the slot.

The trimming of a jib or staysail presents an entirely new problem.

There are some important differences in geometry between jib and main. The first is that most jibs are *loose-footed*. That is, they have no boom along the foot or lower edge. Rather, their clew (their after, lower corner) flies loose in the breeze, free of any encumbrance. The jib has two sheets, therefore, attached to its clew leading back one on each side of the mast. These sheets serve to trim the jib's clew. When you want to haul in the jib for a beat, you trim the leeward sheet. When you want to reach or run, you pay out the leeward sheet. In coming about or gybing (jibing), when the wind comes around to the other side of the boat, you simply bring the jib around with its partner sheet.

The jib's sheets run back along the deck, port and starboard, and through blocks (pulleys) fastened to fittings on deck. These blocks are *fairleads* – meaning that they lead the sheet in a fair line to its termination point – and help provide proper shape for the jib.

Some jibs (or staysails) do have booms, and are usually termed *club-footed* headsails. The advantage of the club-footed headsail is that only one sheet need lead aft for controlling trim. The sheet will have one part attached to a traveller forward which will allow the sail to be manipulated from side to side when changing tacks or gybing. Like the mainsail, when a club-footed headsail is sheeted into position, you can come about without having to tend to the sail's trim.

While a club-footed sail is easier to trim, an advantage to the small crew, the boom on the headsail can diminish its effectiveness as a driving sail in partnership with the boat's main. It cannot overlap (the boom would never swing past the boat's mainmast), and also the boom itself adversely alters the sail's shape.

On a cutter, there is an added headsail-trimming problem: the forestay, upon which is hoisted the staysail, keeps any jib hoisted on the headstay from naturally switching sides during a tack. The jib just gets hung-up on the forestay unless it is walked around by hand.

Perhaps the best solution to this problem – a problem which would be found on any boat with a forestay/headstay combination in the foretriangle – would be a jib with roller-furling gear. With this system, a jib could be rolled on its stay, the boat changed tacks from port to starboard or vice versa, and the jib then unfurled again with its simple roller gear, all without fouling the forestay and its staysail.

REEFING AND ROLLER-REEFING

The method of reefing the mainsail varies from system to system. Older vessels will probably have roller-reefing where the sail is progressively rolled up around the boom. Modern boats will have the near universal slab reefing system with fixed amounts of sail pulled down.

With both systems it is vital to have the sails empty of wind when reefing. There is no point in straining against a sail still trying to drive the boat.

1. Ease the mainsheet and boom vang to spill wind from the sail.

2. Tension the topping lift.

3. Release the main halyard and pull luff down the mast until the reef cringle can be hooked on to the claw at the gooseneck.

4. Tension the main halyard. If the breeze is fresh, you will want a lot of tension to flatten the sail.

5. Pull down on the reef pendant. Normally this emerges from the boom at the gooseneck and will shorten the leech the same amount as you have just reduced the luff. If the sail is shaking with no wind in it, there should be little load on the pendant. If there is, check to see if the boom vang and mainsheet are still loose. Pull the last inch or so of the pendant home, using a winch if one is available and jam off the pendant.

6. Release the topping lift. Now sheet in. The sail can be tidied up. If you have a long upwind beat ahead of you, put a sail tie around the boom and through the reef cringle in case the pendant breaks. If you have tied up the loose belly of the sail, this simple precaution could save it from considerable damage.

Remember if conditions are such that a reef is needed, the crew should of course already be wearing their safety harnesses!

A properly slab-reefed mainsail can be very efficient. Good clew and halyard tension is essential to flatten the sail. There's little point in making the sail smaller if it has a large belly that is continuing to make the boat heel over.

A roller-furling headsail (RIGHT). Any ordinary jib or genoa can be used on the roller furling system.

Changing the headsail.

is often bellied because the leech has not been pulled out sufficiently, and the boom end droops. In rough conditions, the low boom sweeping the cockpit is best avoided. One answer is to roll a sail bag into the leech to reduce the drop. The boom vang will need a claw to fit around the rolled sail on the boom.

Some owners have headsails which can be reefed, the idea being that they avoid the expense of buying a smaller sail. Like the slab-reefing mainsail there is an extra cringle on both the luff and the leech with a row of reef points in between.

There are two main ways to reef such a jib. The first entails dropping it, but the second can be done under way.

The simplest way is to drop it, attach the upper luff cringle to the tack fitting on the stem head, move the sheet up the leech, tie in the reef points, and after moving the lead position on the track, re-hoist.

If you do it under way, you will need a spare jib sheet or the use of the weather jib sheet. Attach the new sheet to the upper cringle on the leech and either bring it aft to a second lead block on the headsail track, or pass it through the lead block in use if the block will take it.

Then rig another line from the stemhead, up the luff of the jib, through the cringle and back aft to a cleat via a block on the bow. The idea is that when the halyard is eased, you can pull on this line and bring the new luff cringle down to the tack fitting.

As before, it is important to tie the reef in, in case a wave fills the bunt of the sail and damages it.

Roller jibs are controlled just like a normal jib except that on one side of the boat a control line will run aft from the drum at the bottom of the luff foil to a cleat or ting sails better than ever to match the gear.

Such sails generally have high clews and appear more like an equilateral triangle in shape to ensure they roll up evenly. They also tend to be cut flatter than normal sails for the same reason.

Roller jibs are controlled just like a normal jib except that on one side of the boat a control line will run aft from the drum at the bottom of the luff foil to a cleat or winch in the cockpit. To unfurl the jib, un-cleat the control line and winch in on the jib sheet. Don't let go of the control line. If the furling drum spins too fast, the control line can jam inside it.

To furl the jib, ease the jib sheet and pull in on the control line. If the line is heavily loaded, ease the sheet more. Rolling in against some jib sheet tension ensures a tight furl. You will need to adjust the lead position on the track each time the jib is rolled in or out.

Most furling jibs come with a colored band on their leeches to protect the sailcloth when they are left rolled up. It is a wise precaution to secure such jibs with a sail tie. Better still hoist a sausage-like sail cover over them for maximum protection.

For roller-reefing the drill is much the same:
1. Release the halyard and boom vang.
2. Take up on the topping lift.
3. Roll the sail down.
4. Release the topping lift and retension the halyard.

Getting a good set with a rolled mainsail takes more practice than slab reefing. Because the leech is longer than the luff and because the luff is held firm by the mast as it is rolled on to the boom, it is difficult to achieve equal tension all along the boom. Consequently, the sail

Spinnakers boost downwind speed more than any other sail. Although they require more equipment and skill than other sails, the rewards are greater. There is no reason for beginners not to set one if they remember one simple fact: problems with spinnakers can be sorted out if the wind is removed from them. Therefore they should be hoisted and recovered in the shelter of other sails, usually the mainsail.

THE SPINNAKER AND OTHER SAILS

There are several types of special sails which can help your boat reach or run more effectively. A *spinnaker*, for instance, is a huge near–hemispherical sail made of light-weight nylon fabric which fills with the lightest breezes and helps push you on broad reaches and runs. You may also use a special spinnaker which has a flatter cut so as to be more effective on a reach.

There are more variants, such as the *reacher*, a sail designed to do what a genoa jib does, but on a close reach, or the *blooper*, a sail used in conjunction with a spinnaker for downwind work.

For all these, remember, there are sheets, halyards, and more. A spinnaker, for example, even has its own spar – a *spinnaker pole* – to keep its windward clew raised, under control, and the sail drawing properly.

Because the spinnaker is the workhorse of all light-air sails, and because it is found on almost all types of boats

from the small-performance planing dinghy to the ocean-going maxiboat, let's take a closer look at how it is used.

First, is any extra gear needed for the spinnaker? Apart from a pole, the other major hardware items are an extra pair of winches. You can use the genoa winches although the extra pair usually enable the spinnaker to be set and dropped while the headsail is still drawing.

The remaining gear is running rigging. A special halyard is desirable as it will oscillate and chafe in a normal sheave. The pole will need an uphaul and down-haul, controlled if possible from the cockpit. Finally sheets and guys are required; lead outside everything to blocks on the quarter and thence to winches in the cockpit.

Small boats, up to 28ft (8.5m), can use just one sheet per side; the one running through the pole end is called the guy. Some means of hauling this guy down to a block amidships is needed to help stabilize the pole. On larger yachts two sheets and two guys are fitted; the sheets lead aft and the guys lead through the amidships block on the sidedeck, although only one sheet and one guy are used in combination at once. The spares, the lazy sheet and lazy guy, are used in a gybe when the sail is set on the other side.

The spinnaker must be packed correctly to avoid twists. This is achieved by running around all three sides, working outward from the head. The head and clews are then held while the bulk of the sail is packed into the bag with the three corners left poking out ready for the halyard, sheet and guy.

The bag can be tied down near the companionway or on the sidedeck behind the jib. It is essential that the sheet on the leeward side and the guy on the windward side are led outside everything before they are clipped on to the spinnaker clews. The pole is then set with the guy running through its outer end and the uphaul and downhaul attached.

To hoist, the halyard is pulled smartly up and made fast. During the hoist, the guy should be pulled back to bring the spinnaker clew to the pole end. The sheet should be slack during the hoist and once the sail is hoisted and halyard cleated, be brought in slowly to stop the luff (nearest the pole) from folding.

There are three prime considerations in trimming:

1. The pole should be raised or lowered to keep both clews level.

2. The pole should be eased forward or brought aft with the guy so that it is at right angles to the wind. If you bear away, draw the pole aft. If you reach up, ease the pole forward.

3. The sheet should be eased until the luff just curls and then trimmed in slightly. It should be played on this 'edge' of collapse constantly.

Gybing the spinnaker is the trickiest part for most crews. Unlike hoisting and dropping, keeping the spinnaker full during the gybe is the secret of success so that the sheet and guy are nice and taut, not flogging away and impossible to catch hold of. In a small boat the pole is 'end-for-ended'; unclip the pole off the mast; clip the pole on to the existing sheet which will become the new guy; now the pole is attached to both sheet and guy; take the pole off the old guy and transfer it to the mast. The helmsman can then gybe the boat and bring the mainsail across. Some slack on the pole lift and downhaul will be needed.

With twin sheets and guys, a 'dip-pole' gybe is used whereby the pole is lowered so that it can swing inside the forestay and out to the other side. Twin sheets and guys are needed to control the spinnaker at all times because the loads will be higher in a larger yacht. As before, keeping the sail drawing will turn a complex job into a simple one.

Make sure the pole is high enough at the mast end to clear the forestay; trip the pole off the existing guy and, by releasing the uphaul, lower it as it swings into the bow; clip the lazy guy from the other side into the pole end; raise the pole on its uphaul. The sail is now flying on its old guy (which no longer has the pole on it) and the old sheet. The aim is to transfer the load of the sail on to the new (lazy) guy and new (lazy) sheet by simultaneously easing the old guy and hauling in the new one: likewise with the sheet. As the process is nearly complete the helmsman can gybe the mainsail. The more hands available the better!

To drop the spinnaker, hoist the jib so that the spinnaker can be dropped in its shelter. The object of the drop is to ease the load off two corners so that the sail spills wind and can be gathered in easily. First either trip the clew attached to the guy by easing the pole forward to the forestay and releasing the snap shackle or, if the guy is long enough, by allowing the guy to run forward. Now the spinnaker should be just flying from the sheet and halyard, like a flag out behind the mainsail. With no wind in it, gather it in as the halyard is released.

This spinnaker (BELOW, BOTTOM) is being hoisted from a sock and is under control all the time. It can be doused at a moment's notice if the wind pipes up.

The consequences of a classic broach under spinnaker (ABOVE). While the sail flogs, the helmsman tries frantically to get the boat under control and prevent the spinnaker from wrapping around the forestay.

STORM SAILS

There are also sails designed for heavy weather – storm sails. A typical storm jib, for instance will be less than a third the size of a boat's working jib, and be made of material at least twice the weight. It will attach to the headstay (or forestay on a cutter) with oversized *hanks*, and have extra-heavy roping, sometimes all around its perimeter.

To replace the main in a storm, there is the storm trysail. This is a similarly heavy three-cornered sail with a relatively high-cut tack and a short clew. Its short luff is hoisted on the mainmast, its tack hauled down to the gooseneck, and its clew sheeted to a point slightly to leeward on deck. A trysail is probably less than one-fourth the mainsail's size.

Not only do a storm jib and a trysail reduce the amount of sail set, if they are cut correctly and trimmed properly, they can also provide enough power to drive to windward and out of danger.

Storm sails should not be treated as a last resort. Not only can they improve the boat's speed in heavy going, but they keep the boat more upright and hence more comfortable. They must be set before conditions have deteriorated to their worst and the crew is at its weakest.

When buying storm sails, costs can be kept reasonable if existing deck gear can be used: spinnaker blocks on the quarter for sheeting the trysail; and either the forward end of the headsail track or snatch blocks on the gunwale for sheeting the storm jib. Savings here can be plowed back into a nicely shaped sail, with triple stitching, reinforced corners and taping along every edge. Other points to look for are metal luff slides, not plastic ones, if the trysail sets in a groove on the mast; doubled slides or hanks at the head and tack of both sails; and wire strops to lift the sail off the deck and clear of waves.

Additionally, if you have a wire-to-rope halyard, a wire strap on the head of both sails will extend the halyard so that the wire comes all the way back to the winch drum, thus eliminating a weak link.

The storm jib is set in the normal way while there are various permutations for the trysail. It can be set either on its own private track besides the main luff groove, or, with the mainsail stowed below the luff gate, it can be hoisted in the normal track. Moreover, it can be sheeted either to the end of the boom, or directly down to the quarter. In most circumstances it is best not to use the boom. Lash it down to the cabin top with the mainsail securely bound up.

The trysail can be stopped by tying very light lines around the leech and through the luff cringles. This keeps it under control until it is sheeted in and the lines break to open up the sail.

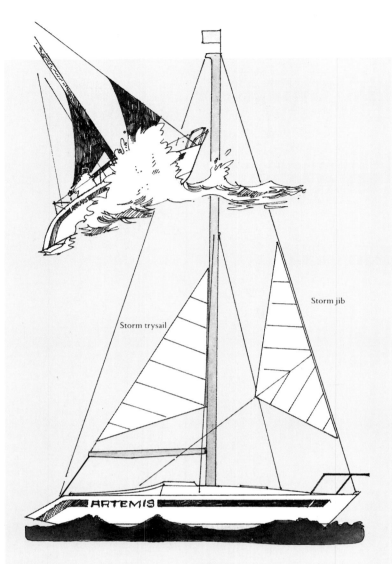

Storm trysail

Storm jib

ARTEMIS

Storm jibs should be of substantial construction with heavy stitching and chafe patches, head and foot pendants and provision for shackling or lashing to the forestay.

A storm trysail ideally will have its own mast track. Be sure to practice setting it in calm conditions and arrange proper leads and stern cleats.

HOISTING STORM SAILS

The time to use storm sails is when your deepest mainsail reef still exposes too much sail to the wind, and when your smallest jib is too big to handle the blow.

Storm trysail In a heavy blow, the mainsail is either taken off the mast and boom and stowed below, or lashed with extra sail ties to the boom. The luff of the traditional trysail is usually attached to the mast with lacings to avoid stressing the sail track, and to allow the main to remain rigged. Some newer systems use the mainsail track, provided it is strong enough, but then the main must be detracked or the rig provided with a track switching system to allow the two sails to coexist. The main halyard is used to tension the trysail's luff, and the sail's clew is taken back aft, its sheet led through a block secured to a padeye on deck or to the gunwale sheeting track. In almost all conditions, the trysail is sheeted flat.

Storm jib The storm jib is sheeted just like a normal working jib, its sheet led aft through the fairlead and to the cockpit. It is hanked to the headstay with snap-hanks, or sometimes hoisted on its own heavy luffwire to keep it further inboard.

Under deep-reefed main and storm jib, this cruiser can still make progress to windward.

Two sheets are required for the trysail and both can be used to give the sail a good foil shape. Modern fin-and-skeg boats need forward movement because their relatively small keels generate lift from the water flowing over them, rather than relying on sheer physical area to reduce leeway.

When attaching the halyard to either sail, make sure there is a large shackle available in case the normal halyard snap shackle does not fit. As soon as the jib or mainsail halyard is lowered, tie it off to the mast, bow or pulpit, so that it is not jerked out of your hand.

Finally, make sure your storm sails are high visibility orange in color and carry some means of identification, such as your sail number.

CHAPTER THREE

SAIL THEORY

Sailing boats move through two different mediums at once; the hull through water and the sails through air. Both components are complementary – a sailing boat moves efficiently if her hull is well designed, clean and fair, and if her well-cut sails are correctly set. Good sails are not enough to transform a slow old hull on their own. There is no point having the raciest looking boat and equipment if they are not correctly used.

POINTS OF SAILING: THE SLOT

The principal points of sailing are beating, reaching and running. Fortunately they are very colorful terms and are easy to remember. You beat into the wind. You reach across it. You run away from it.

In between, there are other points of sailing such as a close reach and broad reach, points of sail in fact all around the clock, except on one bearing – directly into the wind.

Sailing away from the wind is the easiest for the newcomer to understand. Everything we know in everyday life is blown away from the wind, be it leaves on the ground or clouds in the sky.

We call this running away, with the wind pushing the boat ahead of itself. To catch the wind it is logical that the maximum sail be presented to the wind, so the sheets are eased and out go the sails.

On a boat there are usually two sails working in harness: the mainsail and the headsail, or jib. Their total area as well as the interaction between them combine to make an efficient propulsion system.

The gap between the main and the jib is known as the slot and it allows the total force of main and jib combined to be greater than the sum of the force of each individual sail. (We encountered the slot earlier, under **Headsails: The Jib**.) Think of the slot as a channel through which a fluid (air, in this case) flows. A quick look at fluid dynamics shows that when fluid flows through a channel, its velocity affects the amount of pressure it exerts on the funnelling channels.

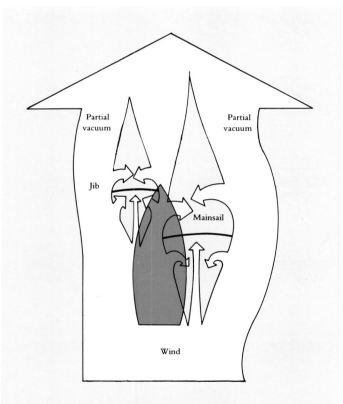

The simplest sailing mode is downwind (ABOVE), where the dinghy is moved along by the airstream and can travel no faster than the wind.

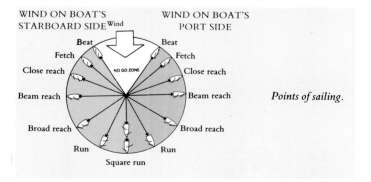

Points of sailing.

When the venturi is at the leading edge of the mainsail, and the pressure drops on the lifting side of the luff, more lift is generated. You also get a bit of extra push out of the redirected wind as it goes through the slot.

Tests conducted in the wind tunnel have shown that airfoils are more efficient when a slot is introduced because it helps guide the flow of air across the back, or leeward, side of the foil. For maximum effect the back of the jib should be level with the point of the mainsail's maximum power, the fullest part of its sectional shape.

If the slot is too narrow, the air is literally choked as it tries to pass through the constriction. The evidence for this is backwinding on the mainsail.

Similarly, a slot can be too wide and the air coming through will be turbulent, instead of the clean, attached flow which is being sought.

SAILING DOWNWIND

The most basic way a modern boat uses the wind is the way the most primitive sailor must have used it: to be pushed along more or less in the same direction – to sail *downwind*. For this, the sailor simply lets the sail rotate out to the side and capture the breeze. The mast, which is securely mounted (or *stepped*) in the boat, and the boom, which is harnessed by its own running rigging (called the *mainsheet*), take the energy the sail captures from the wind and transmit it to the hull.

The hull is level; the wind is acting directly along the boat's centerline; there is no sideways component of wind thrust because the sail is rotated so as to catch the wind almost perpendicularly – so there is no need for a centerboard. The boat is simply being pushed along.

But the wind is not simply 'the wind'. Apart from its essential propulsive qualities it has other intrinsic properties that are potential pitfalls for the unwary, even when merely sailing downwind. Most sailors are therefore very wind-conscious and are aware that there are two types of wind to be understood.

The first is the true wind which literally means the wind which is unaffected by other influences in terms of direction and velocity.

The second is the apparent wind which has been affected by some other factor. Basically, it is the sailing vessel's own movement which causes the true wind to be modified into the apparent wind. Therefore it is the apparent wind which determines which sails are to be set and how they are to be trimmed.

Burgees at the masthead and even electronic wind indicators with their cups and vanes show apparent wind. It is only the more sophisticated instruments that can integrate apparent wind speed and direction with the boat's heading and speed and so can resolve the true wind speed calculation.

When beating upwind therefore, it follows that the apparent wind is stronger than the true one. This is because the apparent wind is the true wind speed plus that of the boat moving toward it. Moreover, not only does the wind appear to increase in strength but its direction moves forward also.

When sailing downwind the opposite applies. The apparent wind is less than the true wind speed because the boat is moving in the same direction and, consequently, its own speed can be subtracted. The inexperienced sailor can be fooled into underestimating or overestimating the true wind speed by the boat's own movement.

This difference between true and apparent wind speed should of course determine how much sail is set. Starting off on a downwind course it is easy to be lulled into thinking how pleasant a moderate fresh breeze can be. With full sail set, the boat will be bowling along until it is time to head for home. Then the boat heels over, cups and kettles crash around below and oilskins are suddenly necessary.

With careful thought this need not happen. The sail plan should be reduced with a reef in the mainsail and a smaller jib set, making the upwind leg as enjoyable as the downwind one.

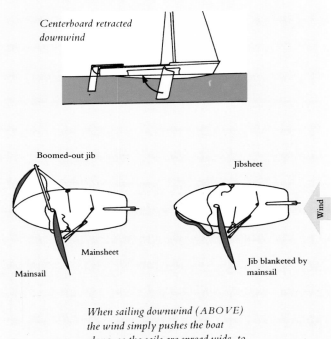

Centerboard retracted downwind

Boomed-out jib

Jibsheet

Mainsheet

Mainsail

Jib blanketed by mainsail

Wind

When sailing downwind (ABOVE) the wind simply pushes the boat along, so the sails are spread wide, to catch the maximum amount of wind while the centerboard is partially or completely raised to reduce any unnecessary underwater resistance.

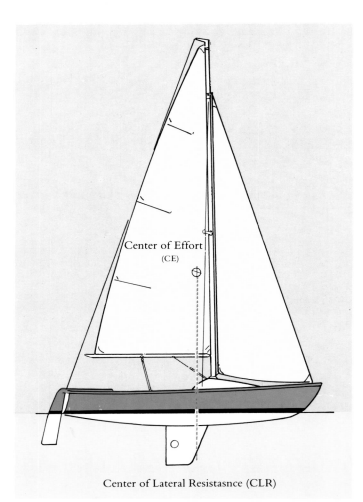

Center of Effort
(CE)

Center of Lateral Resistasnce (CLR)

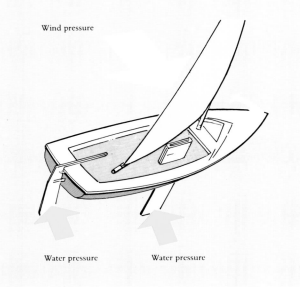

Wind pressure

Water pressure   Water pressure

BALANCE

The way hull shape and sail area interact has much to do with a boat's behavior. This is often referred to as balance, and to sail both fast and comfortably both the hull and sail plan need to be trimmed carefully.

Hull balance is a function of the boat's form. A heeled boat will behave differently from an upright boat. The greater the difference between the bow and stern shapes, the more pronounced this difference will be. A modern design with its characteristic fine bow and full, wide stern can be difficult to handle if it is allowed to heel too far for it will want to turn into the wind. Moreover, the forward force applied to the sails will no longer be above the centerline of the boat but instead out to the leeward side.

So while an older-style craft with narrow beam and long matching overhangs may be more balanced at high angles of heel, the modern design offers a winning combination of space and performance.

The effect of any imbalance is felt through the helm and it affects the steering of the boat in virtually any wind condition. It is the tendency of a boat to try to turn into the wind while under sail. The name of this phenomenon is *weather helm*.

The reason for it is simple. The force on a boat's sail can be assumed to act at a single point, the center of effort. Similarly, all the force of lateral resistance on a boat's hull (underbody, rudder, and keel) can be taken as acting at a single point, the center of lateral resistance. Because the center of effort (CE) and the center of lateral resistance (CLR) rarely line up, but are always offset from each other in a properly designed boat, their forces together form a 'couple' which serves to twist the boat.

To counteract this couple, the helmsman must apply some rudder angle and actually steer the boat against its tendency to sail up into the wind. Because he must pull the tiller to windward, and because the windward side of a boat is also called the 'weather' side, the term *weather helm* is applied.

Some amount of weather helm is desirable. If the helm is left unattended, most boats ought to sail slowly into the wind until the wind spills from their sails. Thereafter they will lie, almost stationary to one side of the wind or other. This is similar to most boat's behavior when no sails are set: most will lie either beam to the wind or stern first.

Weather helm can also be induced by the sail plan. The most common reason is too much sail being carried which just overpowers the boat. The cause may also be such fundamental design errors as the mast being stepped too far forward or the sail plan not being of the right proportions. The mast may have been stepped with too much rake aft.

Lee helm is the opposite of weather helm, ie the boat's tendency to bear away unless checked by the tiller or wheel. Again there could be something wrong with the design but this is rare. If the boat has a fractional rig this may cause *lee helm*. This means she has a large mainsail area and smaller foretriangle. When reefed down, the mainsail may be such a small proportion of its normal area that the balance of the boat is upset.

More commonly *lee helm* is found in light airs. The helmsman might find the boat difficult to steer because the helm is vague and lacking feel. More bite can be obtained by heeling the boat to leeward, so that it goes into a state of slight imbalance owing to the asymmetric hull shape. This, we know now, makes the boat want to turn into the wind, so giving the helm the feel the helmsman is striving for.

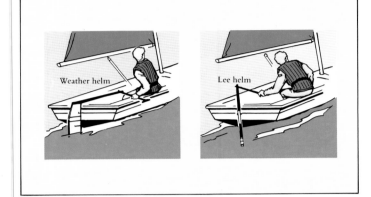

The effect of any imbalance due to incorrect sail trim, crew or centerboard position will be to cause the boat to head up into the wind or 'round up' (RIGHT) This imbalance will be transmitted to the rudder where it must be resisted by applying 'weather helm' (ABOVE LEFT). However, in some badly designed boats it is sometimes necessary to apply the opposite force, ie 'lee helm' (ABOVE RIGHT).

There are essentially two forces (ABOVE LEFT) acting on a small sailing boat – wind pressure on the sails (aerodynamic) and water pressure on the under surfaces (hydrodynamic). It is the rudder's function to keep these two forces in balance.

The center of effort (CE) and the center of lateral resistance (CLR) rarely line up (FAR LEFT). This misalignment causes the boat to turn away from the side on which the sails are set.

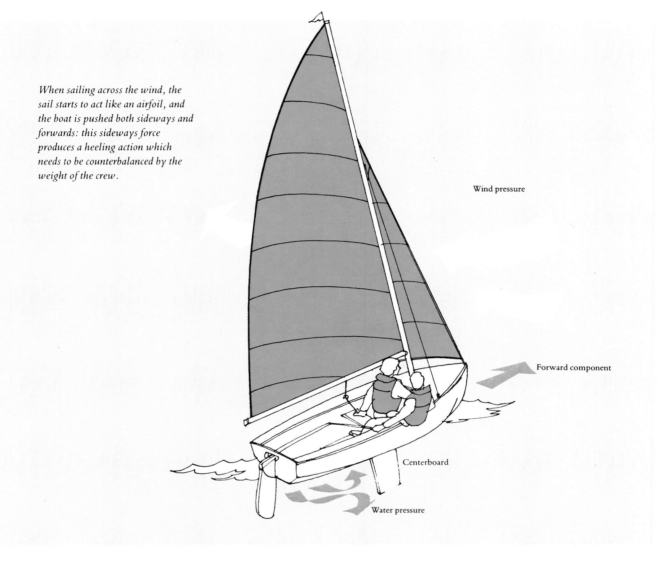

When sailing across the wind, the sail starts to act like an airfoil, and the boat is pushed both sideways and forwards: this sideways force produces a heeling action which needs to be counterbalanced by the weight of the crew.

Wind pressure

Forward component

Centerboard

Water pressure

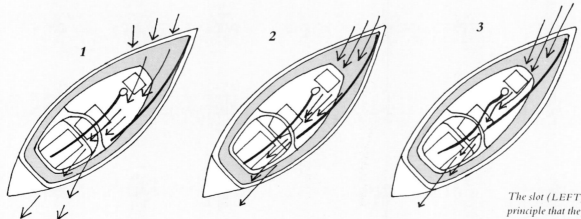

1

2

3

The slot (LEFT) is based on the principle that the field of circulation around the two sails is more effective than a single sail.

SAILING ACROSS THE WIND

'Across the wind' describes a situation where the wind is more or less perpendicular to the direction in which the boat is headed. At this angle, the sail is rotated by the mainsheet closer to the boat – closer inboard. Now the centerboard becomes important in resisting the push of the wind. It digs in and prevents the wind from forcing the boat to slide sideways. The rudder not only keeps the boat heading across the wind, but also assists the centerboard in providing resistance to sideslip. This sail no longer simply catches the wind and pushes the boat; it now catches the wind and partially re-directs its vector with the help of the hull and centerboard. The force of the wind the sail is unable to re-direct acts to tip the boat away from the wind (to leeward). This tipping is called heeling. The sail also begins to take the shape of a wing, acting somewhat like an airfoil in building 'lift' along its leading edge.

Because the boat has a centerboard or keel, the force of the wind in the sails is transformed into one component vector that heels the boat to leeward, and another that drives the boat forward. But the hull itself is also at work. As the boat tries to sideslip away from the direction of the wind and as its keel or centerboard digs in and resists that slide, masses of water pile up on the side away from the wind – on the side upon which the water resistance is acting most powerfully.

But, because water is a liquid, its piling up makes it tend to escape from around the lateral planes of the boat's underbody (the centerboard, rudder and immersed hull sides). Due to the way these planes and surfaces are shaped, the motion of the water as it sloughs off the hull is rearward, toward the stern. A kind of 'squeezing' of the boat's underbody occurs, then, which acts to force the boat forward.

On some designs with more modern foil-shaped keels or centerboards, there is an extra driving force at work. On the side of the keel or centerboard opposite the one with the water piling up, there is always a low-pressure area. In a foil shape, that area is especially pronounced on the forward edge. The lift that's generated on that forward surface helps not only pull the boat forward, but creates a component of force to windward as well.

A sail does a version of the same thing. Air piles up on the sail's windward side, and slides off in such a way as to redirect its energy to create a forward push on the boat's rig. A low-pressure area is also created on the forward surface of the foil, and again, like a plane's wing, the sail develops lift which pulls the boat along.

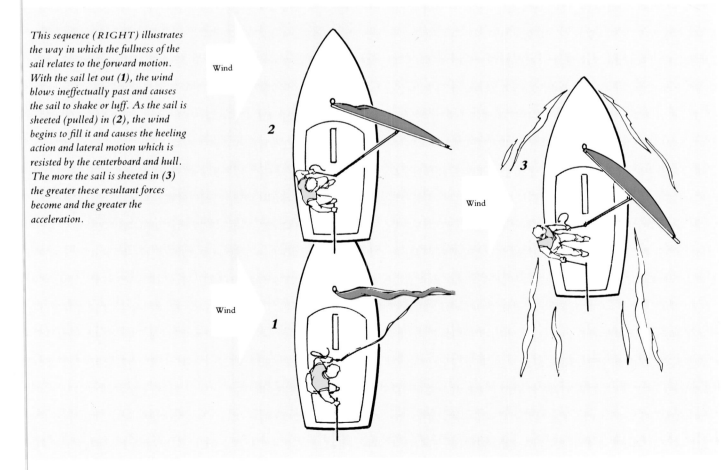

This sequence (RIGHT) illustrates the way in which the fullness of the sail relates to the forward motion. With the sail let out (1), the wind blows ineffectually past and causes the sail to shake or luff. As the sail is sheeted (pulled) in (2), the wind begins to fill it and causes the heeling action and lateral motion which is resisted by the centerboard and hull. The more the sail is sheeted in (3) the greater these resultant forces become and the greater the acceleration.

Wind

2

Wind

1

Wind

3

SAILING UPWIND

It is easy to see how a boat sails downwind by being pushed, but performance across the wind and to windward is often most baffling to the beginner.

Flow across the sails is vital for upwind sailing since they are used to generate aerodynamic lift. Again, everyday objects can aid our understanding of lift. If we hold an umbrella upright in a wind it will try and lift out of our hand. This is because the air flowing over the top of the curved crown has to travel further and is accelerated. This decreases the pressure on the upper surface and the suction effect produced is called lift.

An aircraft wing works on the same principle. The top surface is curved while the underside is much flatter. The accelerated airflow over the top side produces the necessary lift. When more lift is required for takeoff (or landing because speed is reduced), flaps on both the leading and trailing edges of the wing increase the curve so accentuating the faster flow on the top of the wing and decelerating the flow on the underside.

This is why sailing craft cannot sail straight into the wind. The airflow has to strike the sail at an angle so that it flows over a curved lifting surface. Approximately 45° is as close as a boat can go into the wind, although some really efficient upwind boats such as America's Cup twelve Metre yachts can go closer.

This lift converts into forward propulsion owing to the interaction between rig and hull. When the wind strikes the sail it is redirected aft. This causes a movement just as would be the case if you were to hold your hand out of the window of a moving car: slant the hand upwards and you deflect the flow of air, with the result that your hand is forced to rise.

This follows Newton's law that every action has an equal and opposite reaction. Thus wind moving across the sails produces a sideways and forward force. If the sideways force can be countered, the forward component predominates. Hence the boat sails forward.

Imagine a triangular block: if something is placed behind it, to resist sideways movement, then by applying a force (wind) to the angled side of the block (sails) the block is squeezed forward.

In situations where there is a need to steer even more directly into the wind, however, the sailing-boat is able to take advantage of one of its most useful properties, longitudinal symmetry – an attribute that allows a boat to perform equally well with the wind on either side.

This means that when you reach a point where you are running out of sea room, regardless of the angle of your boat to the wind, you can always change course, swing the boat's boom over to the opposite side, and continue on.

Starboard tack

Port tack

Because a sailing boat cannot sail directly into the wind, it can only make progress to windward by zigzagging from one tack to another. Tacking consists of turning the boat's bow through the eye of the wind.

The process of tacking – which we shall return to in more detail later – involves the use of this longitudinal symmetry. A boat can progress toward a destination directly into the wind by tacking, zigzagging side-to-side, with sails hauled close inboard.

HEELING

An inevitable feature of sailing upwind, particularly in larger boats, is heeling, and this chapter on the theory of sailing would not be complete without some words of wisdom on the subject.

A boat is able to sail upwind because the side force is resisted by the keel and hull form of the vessel. But because the hull is streamlined for forward motion the boat moves along the line of least resistance. What side force remains results in heeling.

A parallelogram of forces is at work when a boat sails. Upwind the side force is considerable with relatively little forward drive. On a reach, both side force and forward drive move towards the direction of the boat's travel. The effect is even more pronounced on a broad reach. This is why a broad reach is the fastest point of sailing, because all the forces slant toward the boat's heading and side force is minimal.

How much a boat heels as a result of these forces depends both on the hull shape and its ballasting. As far as hull shape is concerned, beam is the major factor. Following the popularity of racing boats designed to the International Offshore Rule, beamy boats are now common. Beam produces lots of space below decks while offering stability which consequently requires less ballast and hence less cost to the builder.

Form stability is derived from the shape of the hull alone. Its effect is quite pronounced at low angles of heel but as the angle increases so too does the effect of the ballast.

Thus the lower the ballast and the greater its amount, the greater the stability a boat will have. Too much too low, however, is not the ideal answer, for it produces an uncomfortable pendulum-like motion. As in all aspects of yacht design, the best solution is a careful trade-off among many factors.

The resistance to heel is known as stiffness. Any boat of reasonable beam with a high ballast ratio (ie the ballast forms a high proportion of the vessel's total weight) will be stiff, whereas a shallow-hulled boat with internal ballast (common in many racing boats) coupled with only moderate ballast in the keel and perhaps a large sail plan, would be considered tender.

Airfoils (like the wing of an airplane) are designed to produce lift. As wind passes over an airfoil, the windward (under) side experiences a high-pressure build-up, while the leeward (top) side experiences a drop in pressure. This pressure differential is then translated into a push-and-pull force in a forward direction.

CHAPTER FOUR

GETTING UNDER WAY: HANDLING

Before you start sailing, you need to know some general things about your boat and how she responds to the wind and water.

CHECKING THE WIND

Almost every situation will be influenced by the wind and/or the tide, thus being aware of which factor exerts the greatest influence will determine your course of action. As a general rule, it is easiest to depart or arrive with bow facing whichever is the strongest – the wind or tide, the boat will handle more precisely that way.

You should already know from your preparation what the tide state will be at a given time and the direction of the prevailing wind. A sailor must be aware of the wind's direction, strength and how it affects his boat at all times. At first this takes much concentration but it soon becomes almost second nature.

The wind, of course, is invisible. It is simply the air in motion, but how it affects the water can reflect its direction and strength. In fact, the water is a better wind indicator than almost anything else.

Waves are created by the wind, but only certain waves are indicative of the wind in your immediate surroundings.

Swells These are large, long-period waves that travel great distances. Although swells are first caused by wind – a storm at sea – they can originate far away and can travel against 'local' current and wind. Swells that travel inshore from a great distance are often called ground swells when they fetch up in the shallow coastal banks. They usually do not reflect the immediate local weather conditions.

Wind waves Although wind waves are caused by local wind, they can grow into storm swells if acted upon by a large weather pattern in deep water. The wind waves you'll find will be those caused by the wind inshore. Sometimes, wind waves can ride on top of ground swells and act against the direction of a swell, causing a confused sea. Usually, wind waves are the biggest waves you'll be dealing with. Note that wind waves always travel in the overall direction of the local wind. They're the ones that break on top and create those foamy crests called whitecaps.

Ripples These are the smallest of wind waves, and always show the latest trend in the wind's direction and strength. Groups of ripples may appear on the water's surface as dark patches, called 'cat's paws'. By the movement of these dark patches, you can tell where small, localized gusts are forming and in which direction they are moving. Sometimes cat's paws group to form whole sheets of ripples which show as huge dark blotches on the surface and indicate strong gusts.

It is important to learn to see the smallest ripples on the water's surface, even if that surface is lumpy with larger wind waves. Sometimes, the larger waves will reflect what the wind's direction was one or two hours ago, while the small ripples will show the current trend.

For close quarters maneuvering, check for other visual clues: flags or smoke ashore will tell you about the wind; burgees or masthead wind vanes on nearby boats will show if there are eddies or a blanketing effect; buoys and pontoons will show how much tide there is streaming past the point you wish to make fast to.

Flags, either onshore (RIGHT) or on a buoy (BELOW LEFT), provide easy clues to wind direction.

One thing to keep in mind about wind indicators is that they show only apparent wind – one of the two different types of wind we have already encountered under **Sailing Downwind** earlier (see page 35).

The wind can behave erratically, and the most common reason for shifts, lulls and puffs can be the local topography. Land masses can redirect the wind, funnel it, and effectively block it as well.

Headlands can cause the wind to eddy and change direction. Sailing too close to a downwind headland can put a boat in a split current of wind or even a reverse flow or 'echo' off the land. Sailing around a windward headland can put you in a lull, only to expose you to a blast as you get around the end.

Two headlands separated by a low beach can create a funnel that actually 'squeezes' the wind and boosts its speed. The same thing can happen at the mouth of a harbor or within a narrow channel between two islands.

There are also thermal phenomena created to a certain extent by topography. Local wind conditions often vary according to the time of day because of the uneven heating and cooling of the land.

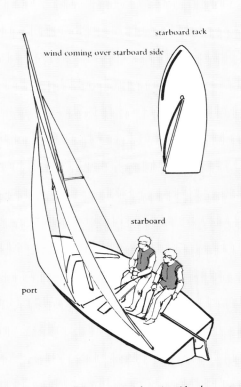

A boat is said to be on starboard tack when it is sailing with the wind coming over the starboard side.

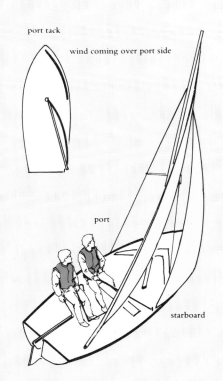

Likewise, a boat is on port tack when the wind comes over the port side.

PREPARING TO SAIL

In a small boat (such as a dinghy), getting ready to sail is actually quite simple, made so by the relatively few pieces of gear that make up the whole. There are the components attached to the hull to facilitate steering and lateral stability, and the components of the rig itself. Let's take them one at a time, in order of typical installation.

Rudder Installed on the hull via its mating gudgeons and pintles. The pintles are normally on the rudder itself, with the gudgeons on the boat's transom. This is sometimes reversed, but the principle remains the same. Make sure to fasten whatever system is provided with any hold-down hardware included, so the rudder is prevented from floating up and off its mounts while under way.

Centerboard or daggerboard A centerboard need only be lowered within its trunk and secured. A daggerboard, on the other hand, must be inserted into its trunk. Many daggerboards have pins that must be inserted to prevent them from riding up and out of their slots. A daggerboard is often fashioned with one longer edge, and this edge should face forward.

Mast Raise the mast vertically over its step, and lower it slowly so that it fits firmly into its socket. Make sure the side designed to take the luff of the mainsail is facing aft. Fasten any standing rigging as necessary, and follow manufacturer's guidelines on rigging tension.

The next two steps can often be interchanged, depending on actually how the dinghy's boom is joined to its mainsail.

Boom The gooseneck is attached to the mast. The boom end often rests in the boat while the end of the mainsheet is attached to the main traveller, and its hauling end is taken through the necessary order of blocks (pulleys). The hauling end is then coiled and stowed on the dinghy's floorboards or thwart. The boom end can then be cradled in its own boom crutch, or supported by its topping lift, or simply left resting in the boat.

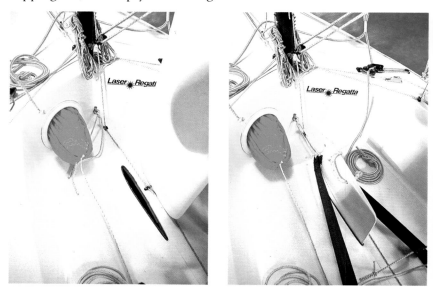

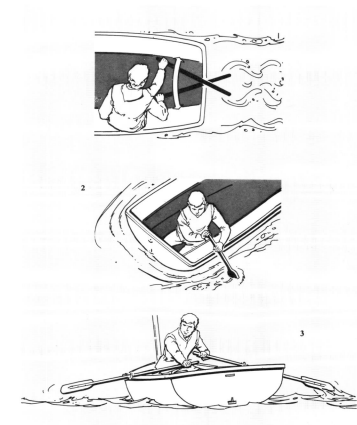

Daggerboards are installed by sliding them into their trunk (ABOVE LEFT) with the longer or fatter edge facing forward (ABOVE RIGHT).

Sculling (1), paddling (2) and rowing (3) are all essential skills.

Most rudders have a simple retaining clip (RIGHT) to stop them from riding up (FAR RIGHT) when under way.

It is at this stage that the mainsail is then hoisted (see **The Sails: Mainsail**, earlier).

The general principles of sailing apply equally as well to big boats as they do to small ones. Forces are larger, equipment is more complicated, but nature remains the same.

But there are some special characteristics that apply only to the larger keelboat: obviously, there are more subtleties to observe, each type of keelboat will show different variations in performance. Suffice to say that experience will soon teach you the finer points of how your big boat differs from your first dinghy.

Remember to do this practising in open water; and let your big boat teach you how she likes to move.

CREW MORALE

Everyone who has spent time in boats knows that things do not always go according to plan, so the seamanlike sailor will not get himself into dead-end situations. He will also not be too proud to abort an approach and have another go. Indeed, the knowledge gained on the first run could lead to a more elegant solution, rather than a clumsy piece of boat handling where one error is compounded by the next.

Prior assessment of the situation and consideration of every alternative action is vital, knowledge of boat handling characteristics and a well-briefed crew, should make maneuvering in close quarters fairly straightforward.

When the helmsman has planned his course of action he should brief the crew. They will need to know where the boat is going, what lines are required and on which side they and the fenders should be made ready.

For their part the crew should query anything they feel unsure of or pass on any information the skipper may have missed, such as seeing a boat preparing to pass close by the destination.

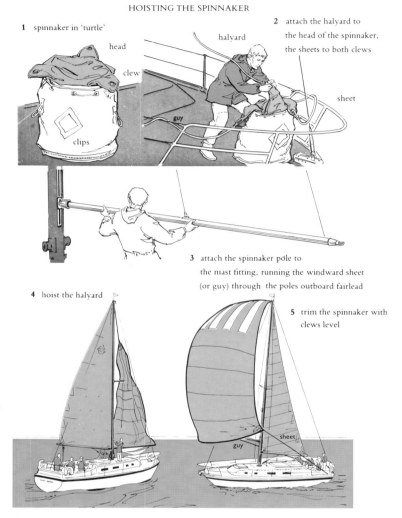

HOISTING THE SPINNAKER

1 spinnaker in 'turtle'
head
clew
clips
guy

2 attach the halyard to the head of the spinnaker, the sheets to both clews
halyard
sheet

3 attach the spinnaker pole to the mast fitting, running the windward sheet (or guy) through the poles outboard fairlead

4 hoist the halyard

5 trim the spinnaker with clews level
guy
sheet

Cleating off the jib halyard (BELOW LEFT) and fitting the battens into their pockets (BELOW).

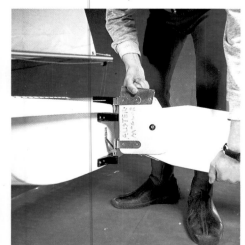

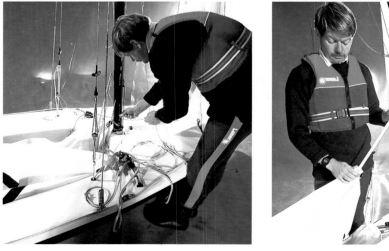

LEAVING BERTH: UNMOORING

Before making any attempt to leave the safety of a secure mooring, make sure you have stowed all the personal gear that you want aboard the boat, as well as the necessary safety equipment, keeping weight as low as possible. If the boat has a deck, the crew should wear a buoyancy aid or lifejacket each. Oars and paddles should be aboard, as should the basic safety kit with its signalling gear. There also should be at least two 20ft (6m) lengths of synthetic line (³⁄₁₆in/5mm will do) aboard to use as towlines should the need arise.

At this point, you are close to being able to run out and go sailing. But first you must learn something about the problems of leaving dry land.

LEAVING A DOCK

For your first sail, try to choose a dock for your departure point. When sailing away from a dock, it is sometimes tricky to get your boat to point directly to windward for hoisting sail. Try to get her to the face of the dock that's closest to being aligned with the wind, then allow enough slack to your sheet to let the boom swing and the sail vane into the wind. Watch the boom so that it doesn't hit the dock or any of its fittings.

Once sail is hoisted, you can push your boat's bow off and trim for a point of sail that will take you away from the face of the dock. If you can't get aligned with the wind, you'd be better off to paddle or scull away from the dock, to windward, and hoist sail there.

In any casting-off maneuver, make sure you know exactly what point of sail you'll be on and how you will want your sail to be trimmed before you actually sail away. Have your route into the clear planned in advance – including where you'll be coming about and how you'll execute the turns and various angles of sail trim – and be aware of traffic and wind gusts just the moment before casting off.

SAILING FROM A BEACH

This is one of the most awkward maneuvers in sailing, and it should be avoided during the beginning phase. However, it is sometimes necessary to launch from a beach or boat ramp.

A beginner should then rig his boat, but he may have to keep the rudder (unless it is retractable) in the boat and the centerboard raised until he gets to deeper water where there is no danger of accidental grounding and he can then attempt to attach the rudder.

Should the wind be blowing strongly offshore – that is, from the direction of the beach itself – sail should not be hoisted at all until the boat is paddled or rowed some

distance offshore, because initial maneuvers could become uncontrollable and some damage to the gooseneck fitting or the sail could result from the boom's swinging too far offwind. The boat should be rowed out, turned toward the wind, and sail raised only then.

If the wind is blowing along the beach allowing the boom to swing out to one side or other and swing free without damaging the gooseneck fitting or sail, then sail could be hoisted and the boat paddled slowly offshore.

Note that the main thing is to get to water sufficiently deep in which the centerboard (or daggerboard) and rudder can be rigged for sailing. If your boat is shallow enough so that you can walk her into water deep enough, fine, but most people prefer to stay dry and row or paddle off a beach. Once clear, all you need do is point the bow to windward, fit rudder (not easy) and centerboard, hoist sail (if you haven't already) and backwind toward the side you'd like the wind on (as in sailing from a mooring). Once the boat is positioned to sail, trim the sheet for whatever point of sail you want, and you're off.

LETTING GO A MOORING

A mooring is a large anchor set permanently on the bottom, with a large-diameter line or chain securing it to a float. A mooring is prone to tide and current, and a skipper must provide a way to shuttle between his boat and the shore. It is still best to practice from a dock first, but the art of casting off and picking up a mooring is a

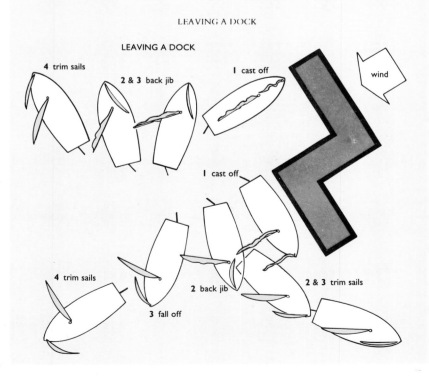

LEAVING A DOCK

LEAVING A DOCK

4 trim sails

2 & 3 back jib

1 cast off

wind

1 cast off

4 trim sails

2 back jib

2 & 3 trim sails

3 fall off

good one to know, and therefore bears covering in this section.

The procedure is quite simple. In most cases, a boat will already be riding into the wind as she sits on her mooring. And, as we've seen, hoisting sail is made easy when the boat is pointed to windward.

When sail is hoisted, make sure to take note of the wind's direction, as it will dictate the point of sail on which you will start off.

Cast off the mooring then pull the mainsail over *toward the side of your planned first tack.* If you want to start on the starboard tack, pull the sail over to star-

board, catching some wind. If need be, push the boom outboard and to starboard against the force of the wind. This procedure is called *backing* the mainsail and is effective in pushing your boat's bow off the wind.

Your boat's bow should fall away to port using the above method. Once fallen off enough to trim for the starboard tack, let your sail back aboard, let it fill normally, haul your rudder amidships for control, and trim for whatever point of sail you wish to use to get clear of your mooring. Obviously, to fall away on the port tack, backwind your sail to port, fall away, trim, and sail off on the port tack.

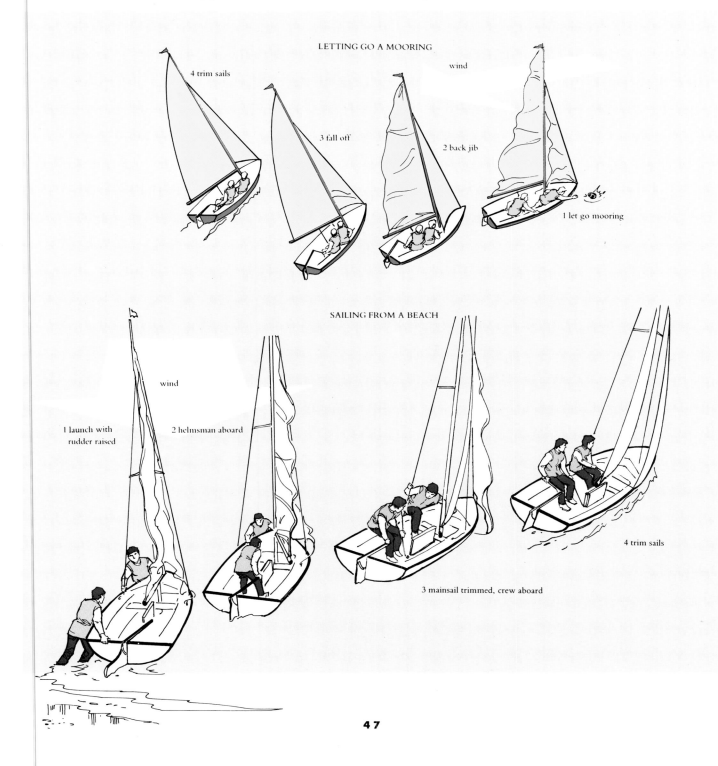

LETTING GO A MOORING

4 trim sails

wind

3 fall off

2 back jib

1 let go mooring

SAILING FROM A BEACH

wind

1 launch with rudder raised

2 helmsman aboard

3 mainsail trimmed, crew aboard

4 trim sails

TACKING

The smallest angle at which a boat may sail effectively to windward is the *closehauled* point of sail, and that angle is usually between 40 and 50°.

A boat may take the wind over either side, port or starboard, simply by changing direction of travel relative to that of the wind. When a boat changes direction so as to pass her bow through the wind and take her sails around to the opposite side, she is said to be *coming about*. If the wind is coming over the starboard side, filling the sails to port, she is on the *starboard tack*. When she's taking the wind over the port side, she is on the *port tack*. Note again that this term applies to all points of sail relative to the wind's direction.

When a boat widens her angle to the wind, she is said to be *falling off*. When she falls off enough to take the wind at about 90° of her direction of travel, she is said to be *reaching*. Between the beat and the reach is a point of sail known as a *close reach*. To achieve this point of sail from a beat, the boat is allowed to fall off slightly. To achieve it from a reach, the boat *heads up* on the wind. Any of these points of sail can be achieved on either the port or starboard tack.

By falling off from a reach, you achieve a *broad reach*, and by falling off so that the wind is coming from directly astern, you achieve a *run*.

All these are simply the terms of sailing.

You are sailing out on the bay, and the wind is perpen-dicular to the direction of travel and coming over the starboard side. The boom, then, is carried by the sail over to port. You are of course therefore on the *starboard tack*.

If the sail is trimmed in tight, flattening it against the wind's force, the boat just lies over and wallows, moving poorly and simply laboring under an over-trimmed press of the sail. The cure is to slack or 'ease' the sheet, to *pay it out* until some of the wind spills off its leech.

When this is done, the boat jumps ahead and comes alive. If you continue to pay out the sheet slowly, you will soon see some wind beginning to flutter around the luff. If the sheet is paid out farther, the boom will trail off to leeward and the sail will begin to flutter like a flag. The boat will also slow to a stop.

When the sail begins that first faint flutter as the wind tries to get around the luff, the sheet is hauled in just enough to stop it.

This is *trimming to the point of draw,* and it applies to more than half the sailing you'll do. It is, in other words, a factor in *reaching, close-reaching,* and in beating, ie the *closehauled* condition.

As you begin to master the reach in a moderate breeze, take care to position your weight properly in the boat.

(BELOW) The 1983 America's Cup winner Australia II on a starboard tack.

Note that the wind pressure heels the boat over to lee-ward, and that the pressure must be balanced with a shift of weight to the windward side.

Mastering a boat on a reach in a good breeze is not easy. It is the basis for all future skills. Knowing how to balance the boat in gusts and lulls and against all wind strengths, and knowing how to ease the pressure of the wind in the sail by luffing are techniques vital to all other points of sail.

COMING ABOUT

(1) The boat is on a reach, on the starboard tack. You now want to go back in the opposite direction, so you change tacks, or come about. Coming about – or chang-ing tacks, or in today's vernacular, 'tacking' – is simply the act of turning the boat's bow through the eye of the wind so that the sails take the wind on the side opposite that it was on when the maneuver began.

Head up to windward at the beginning of the man-euver (2), hauling on the sheet to get set for the moment at which you are on a close reach, starboard tack. Keep heading up (3), hauling even more to get her set close-hauled. It is then that you swing her right through the wind's eye (4).

As you come through the eye, the wind flutters the sail briefly, before she begins to fall off on the other tack . . . the port tack (5). At first, the boat is close-hauled on port tack, but as she falls off further, she begins a close reach, port tack (6). As this happens, pay out the sheet so as to maintain the proper sail trim. Finally, after falling off and paying out sheet gradually, you are on a reach again, this time with the wind over the port rail – the port tack reach (7).

Tacking a boat is the same as tacking a dinghy, but winches take some of the effort out of handling the much larger sails, while the skipper must coordinate the crew.

To prepare for a tack, the skipper should check the area to weather of the boat. The crew pull in the slack on the new jib sheet and load it on to the winch. The call of 'Ready About' warns the crew on deck, and also any-one below working in the galley or at the chart table.

When the crew is ready, the helmsman calls 'Lee Ho' and steers the boat through the wind. The crew releases the old sheet, checks for kinks which might jam in the headsail lead block, and pulls in on the new side.

The helmsman can slow the turn down once the boat has gone through the wind to make it easier for the crew to wind on the winches. He might also luff a little, once the boat is established on the new tack, to allow the crew to sheet home the last couple of inches.

If there is a large crew, one of them can guide the sail around the mast and lift its skirt over the lifelines as it is sheeted in.

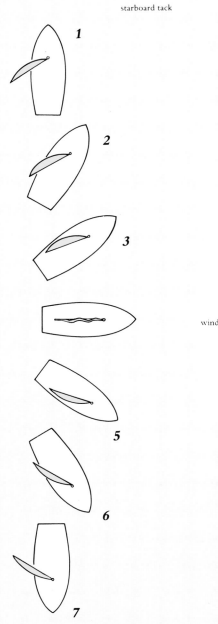

starboard tack

1

2

3

wind

5

6

7

port tack

Coming about or tacking from reach-to-reach involves precise sail trimming at each stage of the maneuver, and is essential practice for the novice. Aim for a smooth transition with minimal loss of speed.

GYBING

Gybing is a maneuver designed to move the boat from one tack to another, but whereas tacking or going about sees the *bow* pass through the wind, gybing requires the *stern* to pass through. Tacking is more straightforward, for both jib and mainsail turn about their captive leading edges (on the forestay and mast) and the wind is spilled from them during the maneuver.

In a gybe this does not happen. The sails stay full the whole time and if they are not sheeted in beforehand in preparation, they will sweep unchecked through a large arc from one side of the boat to the other.

On the next page is an example of gybing in a smaller boat on a reach on the starboard tack (1). Fall off slowly and deliberately so that the boat is broad-reaching on the starboard tack, being pushed along by a brisk breeze (2). You will have shifted your weight slightly inboard now, because the force of the wind in the sails is not as intent

In a controlled gybe, begin to haul in the sheet before you steer through the eye of the wind (4). You do this as you bear off directly downwind. Then, as you steer the boat's stern through the eye of the wind, towards the side your boom is on, trim the sheet in even more, until the wind gets around behind the sail and takes it across (5). Duck your head to keep clear of the boom, and let the sail take some sheet out of your hand as it fills away on the opposite tack after gybing. Pay out the sheet until you are sailing on a run (6), with the boom to starboard.

Note that you should not have to do too much weight shifting during all this, at least while you are aimed downwind. Should you wish to head up to a reach in a good breeze, you would then use your weight to balance the heeling effect. But offwind, the force is not directed so much toward heeling the boat as to pushing it along, so your weight can stay centered. At first, try to concentrate on timing the gybe. The sooner you learn your boat's behavior in a gybe, the easier the maneuver will be.

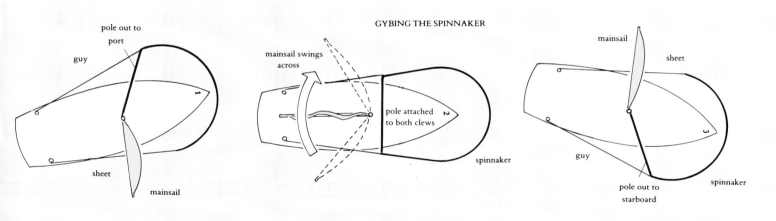

GYBING THE SPINNAKER

pole out to port
guy
sheet
mainsail
1

mainsail swings across
pole attached to both clews
spinnaker
2

mainsail
sheet
guy
pole out to starboard
spinnaker
3

on heeling the boat as on pushing it along.

Now fall off still farther until the wind is directly astern, and the sheet is paid out so the boom is straight off to the port side (3). You are now on a run, your weight more directly on the centerline of the boat, and amidships. At this point, you need only counterbalance the weight of the boom as it hangs suspended off to the port side.

Pay particular attention now because you could get into serious trouble. The wind could get around behind the sail if you turn too much to port (toward the side the boom's on), or if the breeze shifts a few points clockwise. If the wind got around behind the sail, you would hear a loud slap as the sail suddenly filled from the other side and came around hard, carrying the boom violently and uncontrollably across the boat.

This is the accidental gybe, and is something you should not allow. When running offwind, pay constant attention to the wind direction and your sail's position.

wind

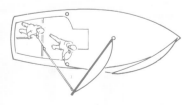

wind

The correct procedure for a safe gybe. 1 The crew tends the jib while the helmsman hauls the mainsheet until the boom is centered. 2 The stern is steered through the eye of the wind and the boom passes overhead. 3 The jib and mainsail are trimmed on the new tack.

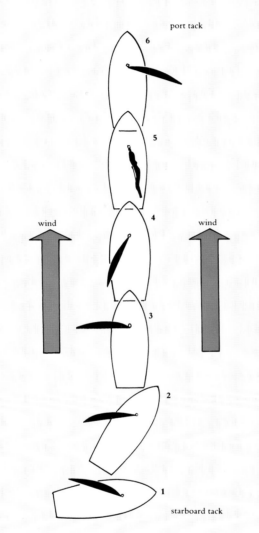

Gybing involves swinging the stern of the boat through the eye of the wind, and the maneuver requires careful control of the boom to prevent it swinging *across too violently in strong winds. Practise the technique in light winds and remember to duck as the boom swings across.*

Gybing is relatively hazardous, to be practised in light winds at first, until the beginner has mastered all the steps in sail-handling and weight-shifting. Controlling the sweep of the boom, in particular, is important as accidental gybes can both injure crew members and damage the rig.

In a larger boat with a more numerous crew the procedure is virtually identical, although the formalities may be rigorously observed: the skipper checks the water he

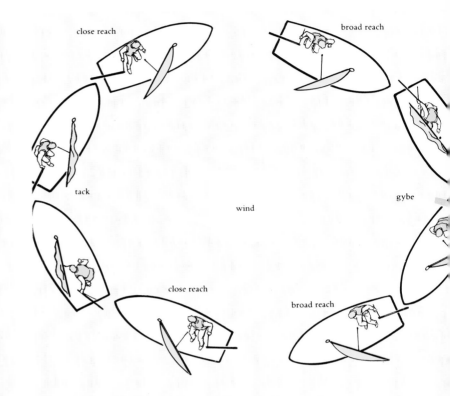

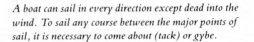

A boat can sail in every direction except dead into the wind. To sail any course between the major points of sail, it is necessary to come about (tack) or gybe.

will be sailing into and warns the crew: 'Ready to gybe'. The crew take up the slack on the headsail sheet not in use. The skipper progressively sheets in the mainsail until it is almost over the centerline. He makes sure the traveller is jammed and with a call of 'Gybe Ho' he gybes the boat, slowing as the boom changes sides.

The crew meanwhile will have pulled in the new sheet before releasing the old sheet to stop the jib wrapping itself around the forestay.

LUFFING

There is one more maneuver which will come in handy during the first phase of the learning process.

Luffing This is the practice of heading up without trimming sail. The wind is purposely allowed to get around the leading edge of the sail and spill off to leeward, fluttering the luff of the sail. This process slows the boat, taking pressure off the rig. Luffing can be used when things get slightly hectic, or when the wind gets too strong for the rig to handle. The sail can be luffed to whatever extent a skipper desires.

AUTO-STEERING FOR SINGLEHANDERS

The most exhausting part of singlehanded sailing is sitting at the wheel or tiller for hours on end. Even if you intend to keep to coastal hops, auto-steering is something you must seriously consider for passages of more than 35 miles (56km). Yet comparatively few boats have been equipped with self-steering devices.

Remember, however, auto-steering does not take the place of a proper lookout. It cannot avoid obstacles. It will aid in avoiding fatigue, however, and permit you to navigate coastal passages with greater comfort and safety. It must be used with discretion and never in congested or crowded areas – moorings, harbor entrances, channels and shipping lanes.

Auto-steering devices fall into two broad categories: wind-powered and electrically driven. Under the first heading come all wind vanes and sheet-to-tiller rigs, no matter what degree of complexity or simplicity they may maintain. Under the second come all autopilots. The important thing to keep in mind when choosing a system is that wind vanes keep course to the tune of the apparent wind, while autopilots follow a compass course, no matter what.

The advantages of one over the other are dependent on the average wind strength in your usual cruising grounds, the time you'll be under power, and the design and balance of your boat. An autopilot can be used with sails alone only if the wind is steady and from one quadrant. Otherwise you will spend most of your time trimming sails, and your fatigue factor will go up. Just what you're trying to avoid.

Yet, in light wind areas, a wind vane, unless very friction-free and reasonably sophisticated (servo-pendulum), will not be able to transfer the wind strength into enough force to steer the boat effectively.

Vanes usually work best when beating, since most boats can be made to balance themselves and sail a reasonably true course to windward. In any case, a vane will enhance the accuracy of the course steered. The vane will, in fact, steer a better course than you, since it is more sensitive to changes, gusts and such. Also, it is always working and will automatically correct all the errors a helmsman might make once his or her powers of concentration have begun to diminish.

Since the apparent wind is much less downwind, a vane will tend to be more erratic on this point of sailing. It is constantly responding to slight wind changes. Thus, downwind, where the boat's directional stability is lessened, the vane will steer from one side to the other. The true course will probably average out, but to an observer ashore, it may well look as if a slightly tipsy sailor has taken the helm.

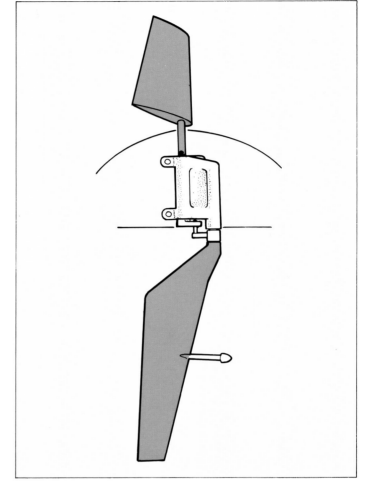

On a reach, the gear will respond in relation to the wind speed. Heavy air will cause – again, with exceptions – more erratic behavior than moderate air. And too much sail up can cause wild gyrations. In other words, the sail power can overcome any mechanical advantage the vane would normally have.

But deciding on which vane to buy is another matter. Much depends on the shape of the hull, the sail plan and the natural directional stability of the boat. Long keels will usually supply a steady helm but make the boat less manoeuvrable. A moderate boat with moderate overhangs, reasonable draught to prevent leeway and a large rudder seems to be the best all-round solution. This assumes you'll use the boat for day sailing, coastal hops, occasional races and offshore passages. No boat is ideal, but the more traditional boat is preferable for such tasks.

If your boat is in the 35ft-and-over (10.5 metres) range you will have to opt for one of the more sophisticated systems.

A final possibility is sheet-to-tiller rigs. A great deal of trial-and-error experimentation is necessary, however, to get them to work.

All wind vanes work on a similar principle (LEFT). The vane activates the rudder or an auxiliary rudder or a trim tab attached to the main rudder. The pressure applied causes the rudder to move and turn the boat. Countless variations exist, with different mechanisms, gearing and configurations. You should discuss the matter with an expert before installing one, because each and every hull has specific characteristics that must be taken into account before fitting any gear.

Some sort of release mechanism for wind-vane steering gear is a necessity for the singlehander. A snap shackle spliced into the tiller control lines with a trailing line led overboard (BELOW) may be the only way to stop the boat should you fall overboard. Little thought of, this is a matter for serious consideration; some means of releasing the auto-steering must be devised. This is, of course, an even greater problem with autopilots; some sort of self-tripping relay may be possible.

The sloop is certainly the simplest modern rig. Contemporary versions tend to have large foretriangles at the expense of the main.

The cruising spinnaker or chute – an asymmetrical, lightweight sail used without a pole for light-air reaching or downwind work – is much easier to use than a spinnaker and is highly recommended for singlehanders and family crews.

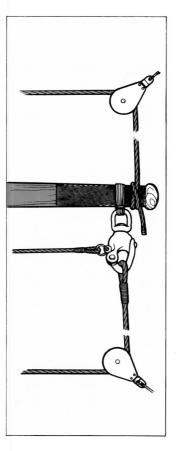

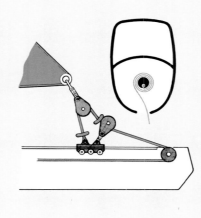

Roller-furling and reefing mainsails, such as the Hood Stoway system, solve the most dangerous parts of manual reefing because they can be totally controlled from the cockpit. However, it also means replacement of the mast and boom at considerable expense.

CHAPTER FIVE

BASIC PILOTAGE: NAVIGATION

Binoculars should be carried aboard; vital for simple pilotage tasks such as spotting and reading buoys. The 7x50 is the most common type for sailing; 7 denotes the magnification power and 50 the size, in millimeters, of the front element. Although binoculars come in many combinations, 7x50 offer the attractive advantage of having well matched entry and exit pupils to allow maximum light to pass in poor conditions. The magnification power is not too great, making it possible to look at objects from a moving platform.

USEFUL EQUIPMENT

A more sophisticated aid is the depth sounder. In most coastal cruising, the nearest land is that directly underneath the keel, so this relatively cheap instrument is good value for navigation. You can buy a depth sounder reading to 325–490ft (100–150 metres) with an alarm which can be set for shallow water, for less than the cost of a set of oilskins. Often there is a choice, in the cheaper ranges, between a flashing light display and a digital read-out. The former can be more useful because the

LOGBOOK ENTRY	Yacht Venus on passage					
Friday 13th April	from: Fairhaven to : Low Bluffs				Crew: A. Morgan, T. Ridley S. Paul	
TIME	LOG READING n miles	COURSE TO STEER M°	COURSE STEERED M°	WIND/SEA	BAROMETER	REMARKS
1200				S.W. Force 4	1001	Left marina, headed down channel. Engine on.
1230	0	85	85	S.W. 3 slight	1001	Engine off at Fairhaven buoy. Sails up. Weather bright, wind decreased. Forecast more wind.
1300	2.5	85	85	S.W. 3 slight	1001	Mid channel buoy to st'b bearing 165° M. Set N°1 Genoa. A.M. very seasick in bunk.
1400	7.9	85	80	S.W. 6 Choppy	999	Wind freshening. N°1 Genoa down at 1345. Steering difficult. T.R. on watch.
1500	12.8	95	95	S.W. 6 rough	998	Low Bluffs bearing 065°. Engine on tick over. Big tanker to port.
	Engine hours 2½ 8 galls					

strength of signal is shown, which may help to show up a returned signal from fish above the sea-bed.

It will also pay to have a simple lead-line as a failsafe back up. this can be used to cross-check the echo sounder. It can be used to 'feel' the bottom and check if an anchor is dragging, or loaded with grease, a lead-line can bring up 'samples' of the bottom. When combined with a bearing, an accurate depth sounding can give a useful fix of your position. For this reason it is best to calibrate the instrument to show the actual depth of the water, not that under the keel or transducer, so remember that there will be less water under your keel than the depth sounder reads.

Another essential is the log-book: either a special book

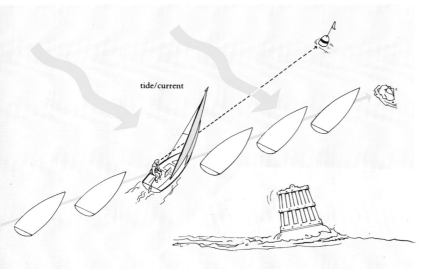

tide/current

(RIGHT) The flow of air which creates a land breeze. Because the land cools faster than the sea as night approaches, the air falls and moves over the water to take the place of air convected off the warmer sea, which in turn falls as it cools with height over the land.

(RIGHT) Katabatic winds. Such winds boost the land breeze. The air is forced up by the terrain, causing precipitation. Cooled by altitude, it rushes down out over the sea.

or just a notebook you can prepare yourself. The object of the book is to record every piece of useful information. As a minimum, one page should record time, course required, course steered, log reading, speed, distance run since previous reading, wind speed and direction, and barometric pressure.

The facing page can contain narrative such as the time a tack was made, when a sail change took place and information gathered in advance such as weather forecasts and tidal data. At any one time, there should be enough information contained in the log to work out the boat's position.

All crew members should be encouraged to record information, while the narrative often provides entertaining reading about pleasures past. The log-book is also a

vital document of record. It may be required as evidence in a protest meeting after a race or to verify an insurance matter.

The log is another vital aid to fixing. By showing the distance run, a dead reckoning position can be calculated. Simple logs are trailed from the stern with a spinning rotator at the end of the line which transmits information on to the log's dial. More sophisticated electronic logs also show speed as well and work via through-hull transducers using devices such as miniature paddle wheels, Doppler effect sensors and ultrasonic sensors.

Unlike the trailing log, onboard electronic logs need careful calibration before use. A measured distance should be run two ways and the results calibrated for any tidal effects. The formula for this can be found in most almanacs.

HELPFUL HINTS

Nobody expects a beginner to burgeon immediately into a sailing master – but a little common sense can go a long way toward making early experiences rewarding and safe. The following couple of tips may be useful.

(1) Try to make your average course trend an *upwind* one for most of your day. It's far better to be upwind of your starting point should you have trouble, than to be downwind with a long row or paddle home. If you cannot sail upwind from your starting point, then try to stay close to home base and that friendly windward shore.

(2) Learn what angle to the wind your boat will tack through on a close-hauled beat to windward. Knowing this will help you estimate what point of land or reference you will be able to make whenever you come about. Looking to windward at approximately a right angle, or 'abeam to windward' will provide a good estimate of the course you can take when you change tacks.

(FAR RIGHT) The navigator's skill lies in relating his own observations and readings from instruments like this satellite navigator.

(FAR LEFT) Try to keep upwind and up-tide of your destination; heading for the mark may not be enough if the tide is sweeping you down toward danger. The effect of the tide on buoys (inset) is self evident.

(LEFT) Typical log-book entries enable the navigator to keep a check on the courses steered by his crew, who must in turn be scrupulously honest.

(ABOVE) When matching the desired course heading on the floating compass card, think of the lubberline as the bow of the boat.

NAVIGATIONAL AIDS

Understanding the basics of navigation is essential before venturing too far away from harbor. Although it is still far from a precise science, the responsible skipper and crew should be able to fix their position if visibility is suddenly reduced and establish if there will be enough water to return to the berth at the day's end.

The single most important item is the steering compass. This should be easy to read with a clear card that's visible day and night. It should be gimballed and have corrector magnets to compensate for deviation on board the boat caused by magnetic objects such as the auxiliary engine.

As the magnetic compass is used both to steer a course and show the heading which has been steered, it is vital that it should be set up parallel to the boat's centerline. The card marked 0–360° floats in a spirit to damp its motion and readings are taken off reference lines called lubber lines.

Correcting deviation caused by local magnetic effects is a skilful job; it is wise to hire a professional compass adjuster to come aboard and *swing* your boat's compass.

The adjuster runs your boat, with all her normal gear aboard, at several known landmarks and along headings he is sure of. He then moves the internal magnets until several cardinal directions line up with the corresponding magnetic directions.

A compass adjuster should be able to reduce or eliminate deviation in the compass. When this is accomplished the magnetic compass rose on your chart and the vessel's magnetic compass are sufficient for inshore piloting.

Once the compass has been swung, always be aware of deviation. Carelessness with knives, drink cans, tape recorders can cause compass error, as can the fitting of additional equipment too close to the compass. Bad land-

falls have been made because of the seemingly harmless can of beer enjoyed in the cockpit and put down too close by the compass. Cross-check the main compass regularly with a hand bearing compass or the known bearing of fixed land objects.

Hand bearing compasses are used to take bearings of objects and are a vital element in position fixing. Modern hand bearers are light, cheap and easy to use. Because they are held close to the face, parallax error is eliminated.

Until recently, RDF (Radio Direction Finding) was about the only electronic means to position fixing in poor visibility. But just as in home entertainment and computing generally, the microchip has brought a reduction in price and now position finders like Sat Nav, GPS, and Loran are within reach of many boat owners.

Given the current pace of development we will undoubtedly see the electronic chart table within a few years. A computer visual display will show all chart functions while the computer will hold all almanac data and process information from performance indicators such as the log and integrate it with a variety of other functions ranging from wind speed and direction to the latest position obtained by satellite. It is quite conceivable that production boat builders will have such systems on the extras list within a decade.

Until then we can choose one or a combination of Sat Nav, Loran, GPS, and RDF.

The latter takes bearing from land-based radio beacons. The great advantage of this system is that it is cheap and receivers can be self-powered from internal dry cell batteries. Great care must be taken in its use for the signal

The hand bearing compass (LEFT) is a useful tool for position fixing.

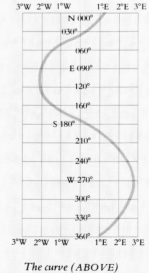

The curve (ABOVE) shows compass deviation, an interesting alternative to the more conventional deviation card with its list of numbers.

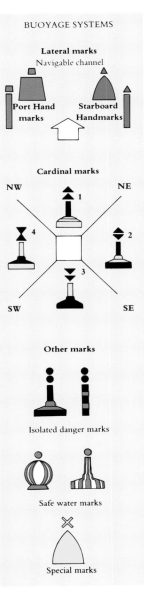

BUOYAGE SYSTEMS

Lateral marks
Navigable channel

Port Hand marks   **Starboard Handmarks**

Cardinal marks

NW   1   NE

4   2

SW   3   SE

Other marks

Isolated danger marks

Safe water marks

Special marks

A marker buoy with a radar reflector (FAR LEFT).

Buoyage systems (LEFT); lateral marks are generally used to indicate the sides of well defined navigable channels. Port hand light is red, starboard is green or white. Cardinal marks indicate the direction from the mark in which the best navigable water lies. They also show bends or forks in the channel. Their white lights flash as follows: 1 Very quick or quick. 2 Three flashes every five or ten seconds. 3 Six flashes plus a longer flash every ten to fifteen seconds. 4 Nine flashes every ten or fifteen seconds. Danger marks have two flashing white lights. Safe water marks are in mid-channel or indicate a landfall, with isophased white lights or one long flash every ten seconds. Other marks use a yellow light. For the significance of shapes and colors, consult the International Regulations for Collisions at Sea.

can be affected by influences on the boat, such as rigging, life lines, atmosphere and topographical conditions.

The shoreside beacons broadcast an identification signal and then a long dash on which a bearing is taken. Almanacs give full details of frequencies, times and identification codes.

Sat Nav gains positions from satellites originally placed in orbit for military applications. Yacht Sat Navs now require far less power than early units and will give fixes of great accuracy virtually anywhere in the world. A fix is updated each time a satellite passes overhead; some areas are better served than others. In between fixes the instrument uses boat speed and course data to give an estimated position, usually shown in latitude and longitude.

In planning a cruise or the course of a race, points along the way (way points) can be keyed into the instrument. This allows it to give you a course and distance from one way point to the next.

Loran (Long Range Navigation Aid) offers much the same with two important differences. One is that it relies on continuously broadcast signals so that fixes are constantly upgraded. This may make Loran a better choice in coastal waters. Secondly, because it relies on ground stations, its usefulness is limited to areas where such aerials are placed. Loran is particularly strong in North America and the Mediterranean, while Decca coverage is found in north west Europe and other areas used heavily by commercial shipping. Both devices also allow way points to be keyed in.

NAUTICAL CHARTS

The nautical chart is the detailed representation of a region's coastal features and sea-bottom contour and composition. It also has the magnetic and true compass directions overlaid in several places.

The chart also has a detailed set of positions for all navigation markers in existence for its region. Buoys and towers and lighthouses and daymarkers – all are positioned as accurately as possible on the chart. Channels are depicted, along with harbor anchorage areas, dumping grounds, commercial port anchorages, and so on.

Many nations have had their own buoyage and light system, each differing to some degree, but all are now connected via a relatively new set of international colors and shapes. Take the time to learn the general rules, as well as the standards in your own cruising area. Learn what the different colors of buoys mean, and how each is depicted on the chart.

Information on magnetic variation is always available to the coastal sailor. A representation of the compass directions is printed on the chart. The compass rose has both true and magnetic directions indicated, with variation taken into account. Therefore, almost all your shipboard piloting can be done using magnetic compass directions.

Charts are the prime source of information and these are available from the Hydrographic Department and their agents and chandlers. Charts must be kept up to date and a service is offered by chart agents although yachtsmen may do it themselves. For this they will need to study *Notices to Mariners*, regular booklets which convey information about lights being extinguished, buoys being moved and so on. Such charts and Notices are mostly produced with the needs of the professional seaman in mind. Commercial publishers also produce charts aimed specifically at the small boat market. Often they cover more convenient areas on the one sheet, or they may be presented in smaller, more convenient sizes.

The chart table (LEFT) must be easy to work at under sail.

Acquire a large-scale chart of the area you intend to visit (RIGHT).

It is part of a navigator's skill to be able fully to interpret a chart like this (FAR RIGHT) in an entirely practical way.

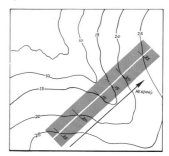

If caught in a fog, one possibility for safe navigation is to follow chart contours. Never trust your senses in fog. Your compass and depth-sounder are your most trustworthy companions.

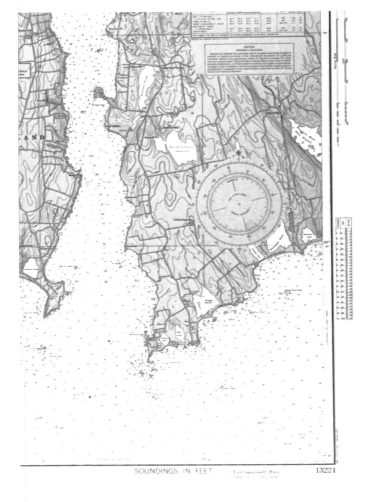

SOUNDINGS IN FEET   13221

area. These tend to be expensive government publications so look out for almanacs which are amazingly good value. As compendiums, they are without match, combining information from many sources. Most almanacs offer a free amendment service so take advantage of them. It is inadvisable to use last year's almanac because a surprising amount of information is revised each year, from port entry signals to tidal data.

Another source of valuable information can be *Cruising Guides* which combine the available information regarding harbors, passages, anchorages and so on, and distills it into a narrative written by yachtsmen for yachtsmen. Harbor approaches are often illustrated with bird's eye views in photographic and sketch form to help the yachtsman assemble information into a three-dimensional picture. Most popular sailing areas are now well covered

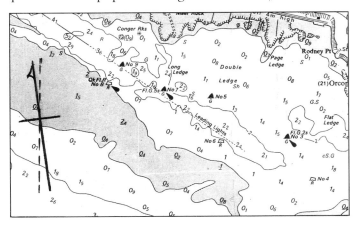

Whichever charts you use, ensure that they are up-to-date. The choice of scale is important too. Scale determines the area covered and also the amount of detail included on the map. For passage making 1:150,000 is an acceptable scale; approaching a port or anchorage requires something in the order of 1:12,500.

The south coast of England, for example, is covered by 10 Admiralty charts in the 1:75,000 scale and they ought to be supplemented with larger-scale harbor charts. It makes sense to stay with one style of chart as much as possible to avoid confusion with differing scales, abbreviations and symbols.

Charts are costly so it makes sense to buy no more than you will need to cover the area you intend to sail in. Keeping them up-to-date extends their life but do not make the false economy of having too few charts. Foul weather can force a change in the best prepared plans so you must make sure that your chart portfolio covers all potential 'bolt holes'.

Other essential publications include tide tables, which give the times and height of tides and a tidal stream atlas showing the flow direction and rate of the tide. You will also need a *List of Lights* and a *Radio List* for your sailing

by *guides* published by cruising clubs, charter boat operators and nautical publishing houses.

As regards equipment, chartwork will require soft pencils, a sharpener, rubber and brass dividers. The most practical type of dividers are those which can be used one-handed. For laying off courses parallel rules are sometimes used, but many small boat navigators much prefer easier-to-use plotters or protractors. The most common type uses a clear plastic square base with a rotating pointer arm used to plot and read courses or bearings. By aligning the base with the parallels and meridians marked on the chart the rotary arm can be swung to read the required course. Such simple use lends itself to cramped chart tables and the quick motion found in small boats.

Navigation is about the elimination of error and making valued assessments of information. A methodical method and tidy workplace help enormously.

Ideally, the chart table should be usable in all conditions and dry no matter how foul the outside conditions. Wet charts and drowned electronics can be a step on a boat's road to tragedy, as errors, inefficiencies and circumstances compound into a total picture potentially more dangerous than any of the individual problems.

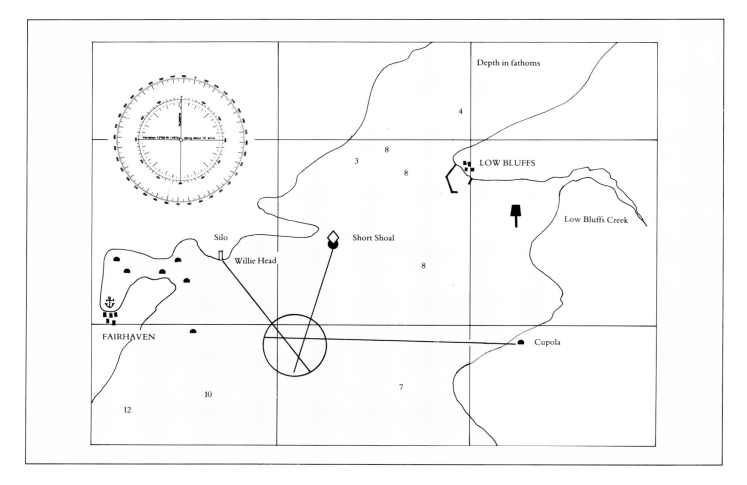

PLOTTING A COURSE

By using a chart and proper piloting techniques you can determine your course, position and progress through your chosen cruising area. This is the most basic chart function. The tools needed for this are simple – a set of parallel rules, a pencil, and a chart.

Example Your trip today will take you from the harbor at Fairhaven to the small creek just below Low Bluffs. There is a buoy just outside Fairhaven, from which it is a straight line to the fixed marker outside the entrance to the creek. Use the Fairhaven buoy as your 'departure' point.

(1) You need to know the course from the buoy to the marker, so you place your parallel rules along the course line, and draw it in lightly in pencil.

(2) Then you maneuver the parallel rules by stepping them slowly toward the chart's compass rose, making sure not to lose the directional orientation of the rule on the chart.

(3) Finally, you bring whichever edge of the rule is convenient to the point at the center of the compass rose, and you read the magnetic direction of your course heading off the edge of the rose, writing it at the beginning of your course line.

DISTANCE FINDING

This is a corollary to the plotting of a course. In order to predict the time it will take to sail or power to your destination, you need an accurate measurement of the distance.

Example You want a good measurement of the distance between the anchorage at Fairhaven and the creek at Low Bluffs.

(1) You use your dividers, the two-legged plotting tool designed to 'step off' distances on a chart. Set them at a short known distance – say ½ mile – and walk them from the anchorage at Fairhaven to the buoy outside, making sure to follow all the contours of the channel. The setting for the dividers is obtained off the chart's scale or from the left or right edges of the chart, where *each minute of latitude is equal to one nautical mile.*

(2) Then, you take a larger measurement from the scale or chart-edge and step off the distance between the buoy at Fairhaven and the marker outside the Low Bluffs creek.

(3) Finally, a few short steps through the channel to the anchorage inside the creek. Then you add all the distances recorded for the total distance from departure to final destination.

POSITION FINDING

Because your chart gives you the exact positions of landmarks and navigational markers, and because you have the ability to take bearings on these points, you can find your position accurately on the chart.

Example You are less than halfway between Fairhaven and Low Bluffs, when the fog begins to roll in and your visibility becomes limited. Rather than rely on an estimate of your position along the courseline you have drawn, you decide to take bearings before the fog becomes distinctly too thick.

(1) Choose indentifiable markers or landmarks around you that can be matched to the chart.

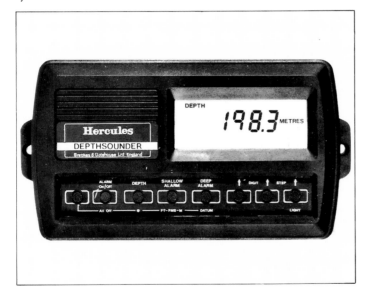

(2) You find the buoy marking Short Shoal and the silo of the farm just south of Willie Head. You estimate that your position puts you at a right-angle juncture between the bearings to these points; in other words, they are not opposite each other, but will provide a favorable triangulation. It is important to try and choose marks that do not fall roughly along a line with your assumed position, for the oblique angle at which such bearings cross will fail to be distinct enough to yield a good position.

(3) You use your hand bearing compass to find the magnetic bearings to both points. Then, after aligning your parallel rules or triangles with the appropriate directions on the chart's magnetic compass rose, you manipulate the rule or triangles to each point on the chart (the buoy and the silo) and draw a line in pencil that intersects your course line.

(4) The intersection of the two lines is your position, but remember that positions of buoys on charts can be approximate.

(5) To check yourself, find a fixed marker (or buoy if a marker is not available) and get its bearing. If your plot of its bearing falls on top of the intersection of the two other lines, then your position is verified.

The position as determined on a chart is called a *fix*.

Several notes: a bearing can be taken on almost anything that is visible on a chart – not just on fixed navigational marks. Distinct land features, shoreline contours, charted structures (like our silo), and other prominent features can be used as long as they are clearly identifiable. Further, it is recommended that you plot at least one fix per hour of travel, even in good visibility.

Readings from the depth-sounder (ABOVE) can be related to the bottom contours to give an idea of a ship's position.

Taking a fix (LEFT). Compass bearings to silo on Willie Head, tower on Short Shoal, and cupola on far shore, when laid down on a chart, produce a set of crossing lines. The fix is inside the triangle made by the inter-section of the lines.

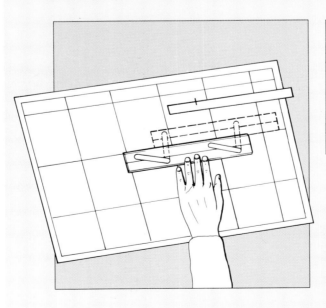

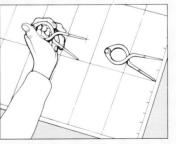

Transferring position lines using a parallel rule (LEFT). All distances are taken (with a pair of dividers) from the adjacent latitude scale at the side of the chart being used (ABOVE).

DEAD RECKONING

This refers to the logical computation of course, speed, and distance as transferred from full-scale to chart and the reverse.

There are many things to take into account when creating a dead reckoning plot, and the more you know, the better your plot will be.

* Boat speed: of course, you need to know what speed you are making through the water. A speed indicator such as sumlog is a good device for measuring. You can also take fixes and compute your personal speed between them by a simple time/distance calculation. The projection of this calculation is useful in dead reckoning as long as other factors remain unchanged. These factors would include:

* Tidal stream: the strength (its speed in knots), and the direction in which it flows, and the times of its change in each area.

* Wind: its direction and strength.

THE DR PLOT

The basic method for setting up a dead reckoning plot is to draw your course line or lines, then predict your speed capability for each leg of the plot according to what you know about your boat's own character, the expected prevailing wind conditions and the rate and direction of the tidal stream.

Example You are continuing along a course to Low Bluffs, after having fixed your position. The fog has drifted in, and although you can see a great deal of water around you the shoreline is obscured. Your job is to continue along, predicting when you will arrive at the several buoys along the way, and when you will arrive at the final destination.

(1) Examine the tidal stream information printed on the chart (marked by diamonds at various key points on the chart) and relate them to the times of High Water. If the chart does not provide tidal information, check a tide table. You may find that you have a tidal stream of 2 knots helping you along in the direction of travel. Unfortunately, that stream will drop off and soon change against you – in perhaps two hours. For now, though, add 2 knots to the speed indicated on the sumlog to get the actual speed over the bottom.

(2) You compute your speed by determining the time it took to travel from your departure point outside Fairhaven to your recent fix.

$$\text{Knots} = \frac{\text{Distance (nautical miles)}}{\text{Time}}$$

(3) Project your present speed and course along the line on the chart, accounting for the favorable current.

Each hour of progress is noted with a tick in pencil along the course line labelled with the 'DR' (dead reckoning) time of arrival at that point. Ex: 0900 DR, 1000 DR, 1100 DR, and so on.

(4) At regular intervals, you may need to adjust the DR plot. Things to take into account will be: change in sumlog-indicated speed; change in tidal stream; wind shift.

TIDAL STREAM VECTORS IN DR

Note that when the tidal stream in our above example changes in a few hours, it will come directly against us. If its speed is listed at 2 knots on the chart or in the tide and current book, then you will lose a 2-knot boost and pick up 2 knots' worth of resistance to your forward motion over the bottom. That means a four-knot difference in speed to figure-in to your DR from the estimated time of current change.

However, as with all things, there are more complex situations, like cross tides.

Example If the current shifts so as to present itself from one side or the other of the direction of travel, then it will act to move you sideways, or set you, and you must compensate for its action by a corresponding change in course.

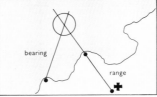

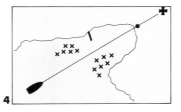

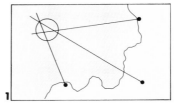

(1) A good triangulation gives a reliable fix. (2) Angles which are too narrow give an unreliable fix. (3) A range and a bearing give a good fix. (4) A range sited to keep approaching boats away from isolated dangers such as rocks.

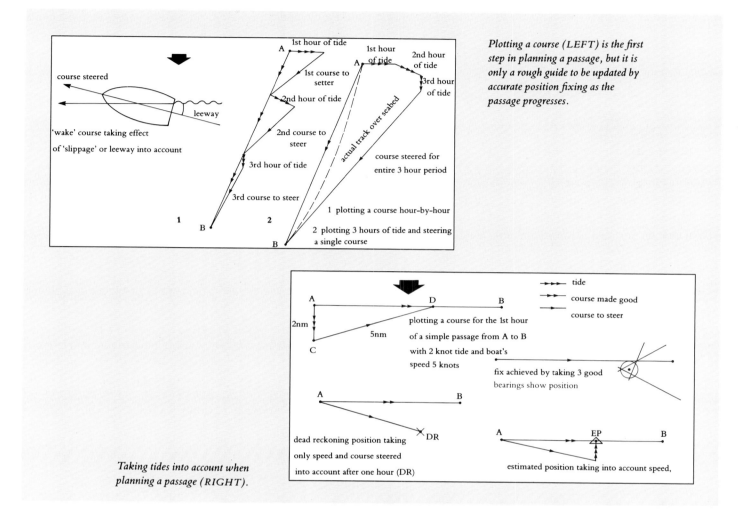

Plotting a course (LEFT) is the first step in planning a passage, but it is only a rough guide to be updated by accurate position fixing as the passage progresses.

Taking tides into account when planning a passage (RIGHT).

(1) The best way to figure course-compensation for a shift of current outside our course line is to draw a vector diagram. An arrow of a length to represent the boat's speed is drawn, and another to represent the current's relative direction and speed is drawn. A third line is drawn from the base of the boat's arrow to the base of the current's arrow. The angle formed between the boat's arrow and this third line is the angle and direction of the compass-heading change required to maintain present course while accounting for the current's set.

(2) In addition to a heading change as noted above, there will also be a change in real boat speed. The third arrow may be thought of as representing *time*. In the example, the first arrow was drawn five scale nautical miles long to represent a speed of five knots (five nautical miles per hour). The second line expressed a current of two knots coming at right-angles from the starboard side. The third arrow, extended from the base of the boat's arrow to the base of the current's arrow, was longer. Its new length, when compared to the length of the first arrow, shows the percentage of increase in time it will take to travel five nautical miles.

(3) Note that the third arrow also may be thought of as representing speed, whereby to compensate for an adverse tidal stream and maintain both the original DR course and speed, the boat's speed through the water must be increased.

The sailor will either estimate the percentage or calculate it and apply the time differential to the boat's speed, reducing it. An easy example: the third arrow turns out to be one fifth longer than the first – meaning that the 5 nautical miles will take 12 more minutes to cover on the current-compensated heading. Or . . . the boat is now travelling one-fifth as fast, or at a speed of 4 knots.

Spend some time familiarizing yourself with vector problems, and learn to apply the time/speed/distance relationship – particularly with tidal vectors. You will soon be able to apply what you've learned to almost any DR situation involving the several outside forces affecting your boat. If she makes leeway under sail, or if the tidal stream in your area is particularly strong or variable, then a vector estimate to quantify it will go a long way towards improving your DR plotting.

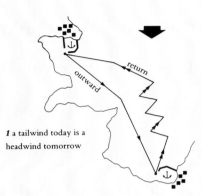

1 a tailwind today is a headwind tomorrow

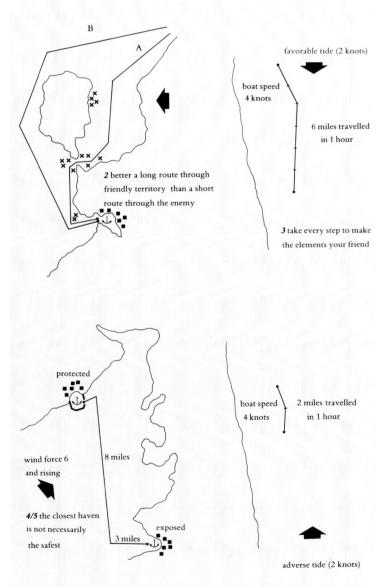

2 better a long route through friendly territory than a short route through the enemy

3 take every step to make the elements your friend

4/5 the closest haven is not necessarily the safest

USING THE CONDITIONS

Better materials and refined technology and design have replaced the old ways, and the modern cruising boat is weatherly and capable in rough going.

Make a habit of listening to the regularly scheduled weather forecasts, and log them in your log-book morning and evening, and to back up the official reports, take three daily readings on your own barometer, noting both the pressure and the trend and degree of change. Log these indicators as well.

By monitoring the radios, and keeping a good log, you will have that much more information at the ready if and when it is needed in a decision.

There are several good common sense rules to bear in mind when making a trip of any duration, long or short.

(1) *A tailwind today is a headwind tomorrow.* A fine downwind start in the normal prevailing winds of summer, can mean a hard push back upwind at the end of a cruise. Because a beat to weather takes much longer than a nice broad reach or run, learn to allow time for it.

Note your weather reports. Listen for cyclic changes in wind. Often, when a front moves through, the wind can veer or back halfway around the compass from its normal direction. You may be able to take advantage of this and make a fair sail for home.

(2) *Better a long route through friendly territory than a short route through the enemy.* If the wind favors one side of a passage, even if the way is longer, it is best to take it.

Stay away from lee shores in a blow; hug those shores that serve to block a strong and unfavorable wind.

(3) *Take every step to make the elements your friend.* If you have a contrary wind, try to make the tide your ally; and vice versa.

If waiting a few hours will get the tide in your favor, then wait. But if that wait puts you in danger of being caught out in that afternoon squall, then maybe you should go now. Weigh the options carefully.

(4) *There is no shame in retreat.* You may be halfway home, and a big blow can threaten to close your passage. Turning back to your previous port may be the only answer. However:

(5) *Any port in a storm.* More sailors find more new ports-of-call this way. If the weather threatens to close your passage and stop your forward progress, check your chart for a harbor close enough and protected enough to offer sanctuary. Look for good holding ground for your anchor (mud, silt, soft sand), and land that is high enough to offer at least some wind protection.

A harbor entrance with sand bar (FAR LEFT) demands precise navigation.

Under sail off the coast of Yugoslavia.

ANCHORING

Anchoring is another form of mooring, where instead of picking up a fixed ground chain the boat uses her own equipment to lay a mooring. This can be in a busy harbor, quiet roadstead or perhaps a deserted bay where the scenery allows you to enjoy one of the great satisfactions of sailing.

Above all, anchoring is fundamental to a boat's safety. It can provide an opportunity to deal with a problem, such as engine failure, or it can enable you to wait for adverse tidal or weather conditions to change to your advantage.

THE ANCHOR

The anchor itself has some major components: the *shank* is the shaft to which the anchor line, or *rode*, is attached by stout shackle. The *crown* is the end that attaches to the bottom, the *flukes* being the broad 'shovels', attached to the crown, that dig in. Generally, an anchor has a cross-piece to help it orient itself on the bottom so as to dig its flukes in; this piece is called the *stock*.

With many boatbuilders supplying an anchor plus a

This plow is stowed on the stemhead roller ready for instant use.

chain and warp as standard you may not be faced with choosing an anchor but it is seamanlike to carry a second anchor, a kedge, and often a different type provides a choice should the main anchor fail to hold. When choosing an anchor for your boat you will need to match the boat's displacement with the anchor manufacturer's recommendations.

There are many different types of anchor, each suited to a different bottom consistency and purpose.

(1) *Danforth* This is the world's most common anchor. It is a good general purpose anchor, designed to orient itself properly on whatever bottom it finds. It does this by catching the bottom with either of two short flukes on its crown. These short flukes serve to rotate the large flukes downward, toward the mud or sand of the bottom. The anchor then digs its way in as the boat powers astern with tension on the rode. Because a Danforth is so well designed, it does not need to be quite as heavy as other types, and therefore is ideal for smaller boats with small crews.

(2) *CQR or plow* The CQR is a rather heavy anchor that uses its weight to orient itself properly on the bottom. It has a single plow-like fluke attached by a spin swivel to its stockless shank. The weight of the large fluke, as well as the shape of its edges, work the anchor into the bottom. The CQR type is good for rocky or coral bottoms, as its sharp fluke easily catches outcroppings or snags. However, it also works nicely in sand or mud. Its biggest advantage is that it is housed easily on a short sprit at a boat's bow. Many boats carry both a Danforth and a plow.

(3) *Yachtsman or standard fisherman's* The yachtsman anchor is the simplest and one of the oldest designs available today. It is often called a *kedge* because it can be set – by simply dropping it, using its weight to bury into the bottom – and hauled upon to work a boat off a grounding. The yachtsman is among the heaviest of all anchors. But perhaps that is why it remains popular, even in competition with the newer high-tensile lightweights. Its weight is as much a factor in its holding power as any design feature. Because its stock is at right-angles to its flukes, the flukes are able to dig in. However, only one fluke

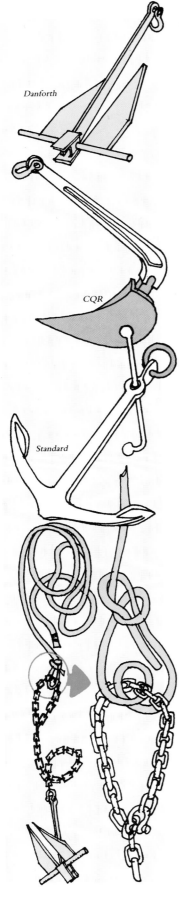

Danforth

CQR

Standard

ever finds bottom, and it is a narrow one at that. This makes the yachtsman anchor good in hard mud, hard sand, gravel, or a mixture of gravel and weed – places where a Danforth could be less than ideal.

While CQR anchors must all be housed in bow chocks, Danforths may be brought up on deck and laid flat in deck mounts or stowed below. Yachtsman anchors can be partially dismantled (by rotating their stocks) and stowed flat in deck mounts.

OTHER ANCHORING EQUIPMENT

The anchor, of course, is important, but so are the other components. Line, deck fittings, chain and shackles are among the other pieces of hardware involved.

The anchor rode can be of rope or chain. Chain is heavier and much more expensive but is preferable. This is because its own weight helps lower the pull on the anchor as well as acting as a damper as the boat surges against the anchor. Chain also self-stows, in that it hardly ever tangles as it is fed into its locker.

Rope however is cheaper. It also suits the modern style of boat which has fitted-out forecabins with berths rather than the old style fo'c'sle which was used just for stowage, not as a sleeping cabin. Nowadays, foredeck lockers are often used to stow the anchor. Rope is also used because the modern fine-bowed boat does not like weight in the bow. It is detrimental to performance.

Whether you choose rope, chain or a combination of both, be sure to mark it properly in either fathoms or feet. In the old days chain was calibrated and marked with leather thongs but today paint will suffice. On rope, whipping twine can fulfill the same function. It is important to know how much you have paid out.

An anchor must be securely lashed, whether to the pulpit, deck fittings or a stemhead roller. The damage caused by a loose anchor is frightening to contemplate.

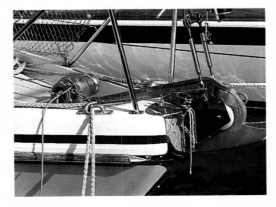

The CQR (Plow, etc.). The original was designed in 1933 to anchor Flying Boats and the name is a corruption of 'secure'. This type affords excellent holding on all types of bottom except thick-weed. Should it drag, the clever design allows the anchor to plow itself in again. Many consider the genuine forged CQR the finest anchor available for most circumstances.

it is easy to add a rope on to the chain should you need to lengthen the anchor rode.

Although handling the anchor is hard work it can be made easier by stowing the anchor permanently on the bow roller, or by having a windlass, or a combination of both. If the anchor remains on the roller it must be firmly secured so that it does not come adrift and damage the boat whilst under way. A lock pin through the shank and several stout lashings should do the job.

A windlass is a boon even for a moderate size anchor and chain, though it is of less use if rope is used. It can be manually or power operated. Often windlasses have one ribbed winch drum, or gypsy, for rope and another notched drum for chain. If they can be operated independently, so much the better.

Anchor rode should be led below through a *deck* or *hawse pipe guarded from water intake by a cap that allows the line to feed out.* Finally, stout hardware on the foredeck must be sized suitably for the ground tackle a boat needs. Deck cleats must be large enough to handle the strain and diameter of line used. *Fairleads* must be of a size to handle the diameter of line and must lead the line clear of any obstructions on deck.

Perhaps the best anchor or mooring connection on any boat's foredeck is a *samson post.* This is a post that penetrates the deck itself and mounts deep inside the boat, down in the structure of framing forward. It gains tremendous strength by tying into the boat thus, and therefore provides the best purchase for anchoring, as well as for towing. The upper end of a samson post can carry a windlass or a single crossbar for belaying the rode.

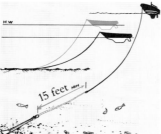

A well planned foredeck (FAR LEFT), with anchor, windlass, bollard, two fairleads and large cleats.

Always allow for tidal range when anchoring (LEFT). With a chain and rope rode, a reasonable length of chain is necessary to prevent chafe and add weight to the catenary.

It is essential that the bitter-end, the end attached to the boat, should be secured firmly to a strong part of the vessel. A small U-bolt in the bow well is not strong enough. Whether the bitter-end is attached in the well or if the chain is led belowdecks via a navel or hawse pipe, be sure to use rope and not a shackle. Rope can always be cut in an emergency, such as another boat fouling your anchor and dragging your boat into danger, whereas a shackle cannot. If you stow your chain below deck, it helps to have this rope fastening long enough to allow the last link in the chain to emerge on deck. In this way

ANCHORING

To set the stage for dropping anchor, a skipper first must find a proper spot. In the beginning, this will take much thought, but after a while, you will get better at picking the best location.

There are some basic criteria for locating the best anchoring position:

(1) *Protection* A harbor with high ground in the way of the wind's direction. Or a spot with a harbor best sheltered from the weather.

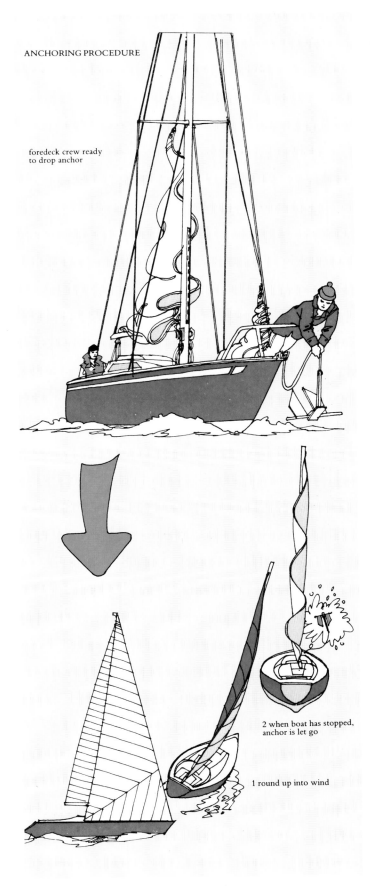

ANCHORING PROCEDURE

foredeck crew ready
to drop anchor

2 when boat has stopped,
anchor is let go

1 round up into wind

*Anchor is down, but the
crewman can feel it dragging*

(2) *Depth* A spot with enough depth to accommodate a vessel's draft at mean low tide, and with enough depth all around within a circle whose radius is described by the boat's anchor rode. Depth can be determined by examining the soundings on a chart, and then by testing the exact location with electronic depth-sounder or weighted line *(leadline)*.

(3) *Holding bottom* A spot with the proper bottom characteristics for the anchor being used.

(4) *Swinging room* A spot clear enough of other boats and natural obstructions to allow 360° swinging around the anchor, within a circle whose radius is described by the boat's anchor rode. And a spot that permits enough anchor rode for secure holding. A skipper should look at all the other boats within the anchorage and determine which of them have similar characteristics to his own. Other sailing boats make better neighbors than powerboats do, as sailing boats will respond to tidal stream more readily (because they have deeper keels), and powerboats will respond to wind (because they have less in the water and more superstructure).

As in many aspects of sailing, preparation goes a long way to making difficult tasks simple. Having made your assessment of where to anchor, brief the crew. Work out a simple system of hand signals so that helmsman and foredeck hand can slow the boat down, stop, go left, right or astern and let go the anchor without shouting or confusion. This can help the family crew, where father might give the helm over to mother so that he can handle the heavy work forward.

Next, prepare the chain or rope. This can be flaked out on deck or in the well. If you are using all chain you will need three to four times the depth of water and six to seven times if you are using rope with just a little chain. In rough conditions, more scope will be needed.

Scottish solitude.

The following are the steps for the procedure, using one anchor:

(1) *In position* The skipper brings the boat up into the wind, either under sail or power. If under sail, he must allow himself the room to sail away again if the anchor fails to bite and the boat drifts too close to other anchored boats. For this reason, it is generally considered wise for the beginner to anchor under power during the learning stages.

Under sail, the boat must coast to a stop at the position where the anchor is to be dropped; under power, the engine is reversed and the boat stopped. When over the drop point, the boat should be pointed directly to windward.

Note that sometimes other boats will be lying with their bows towards the direction of the *tidal stream* rather than the wind. In such a situation, sailing up to anchor becomes more complicated and less desirable.

(2) *Letting go* The foredeck crew then lets go the anchor, letting it down so as to keep the rode clear of the anchor's stock and flukes. Once the anchor is on the bottom, the crewman signals the helm.

(3) *Backing down* The engine is then reversed; or the boat begins to drift astern with the wind on her rig pushing her. If under sail, the jib is dropped, and the main is sheeted loosely so as not to fill. As the rode comes taut, the bowman lets it slip from his grip, applying a slight tension. Once the anchor is approximately one boatlength away, the bowman gives the rode a sharp tug to get the anchor positioned in the correct attitude. The boat continues to back.

(4) *Allowing enough scope* Scope is the amount of rode let out. It is important to pay out a scope that is correct for the depth of the water. Experts agree that a ratio of seven-to-one is appropriate for most conditions. That is, seven feet of rode for each foot of depth, from the *foredeck to the bottom,* taking into account the change of tide. If possible, always set out enough scope for *high tide.* The easiest way to determine correct scope is to take note of the approximate distance the anchor falls before it strikes bottom, then multiply by seven. As you become more experienced, you will learn to gauge scope by looking at the angle of your anchor rode as it becomes taut at the bow.

(5) *Setting the anchor* Just before the proper scope is achieved, the bowman should take a wrap of rode on the windlass capstan or the bow cleat or post. He then should take some strain, slowing the boat's rearward motion. He will feel the anchor begin to dig in as he applies pressure. If the flukes are skipping on the bottom, he will feel short tugs on the line; if the anchor is digging, he will feel a steady increase in pressure. When he feels the anchor bite, he must take more turns on the fitting to stop the rode from paying out.

SOME POINTS TO CONSIDER WHEN ANCHORING

Allow for swinging room and for reversal of position when tide changes. In areas of vast tidal range, with swift inrushing tides, such as Brittany or Newfoundland, where ranges can be upward of 30 feet (9 meters), you will have to anchor far out with a large amount of scope.

Bottom composition can be determined by depth sounder, chart reference or hand lead armed with tallow or grease. The bottom may determine the type and size of anchor you set.

Too often anchors are tossed, dropped or slung over the bows. By carefully and slowly lowering it you will be able to ascertain the rate of drift, and will avoid permanently damaging the hull, deck or yourself.

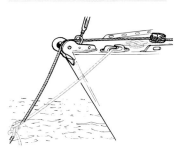

One possible method of securing the rode as well as taking strain off the line is shown here (ABOVE). Deck cleats must be very strong to allow this maneuver.

Hoisting the anchor – a job for strong arms and straight backs.

If the maneuver has been done under sail, it is completed, no further procedures for keeping the boat in motion are necessary and sail may be taken down and furled. But if you've anchored under power, the engine should be reversed again and run in reverse for several minutes to make sure the anchor has hooked itself firmly in the bottom.

(6) *Taking bearings* When all is secure, it is wise to take a set of anchor bearings. These can vary from a formal set of compass bearings on fixed shoreline features, to a casual lining up of landmarks and other boats. In the middle of the night and during a squall, a skipper must be able to glance about and determine if he's dragged anchor and changed position.

1

2

3

*With plenty of room to maneuver, this cruiser sets her mainsail (**1**) and sails up to her anchor which is*

*retrieved by the crewman on the foredeck (**2**). Once clear of the water, the crewman signals to the*

*helmsman that he is free to bear away (**3**) and order the jib to be set.*

TWO ANCHORS

There are occasions when it is wise to put out more than one anchor. Strong shifts of wind can cause one anchor to pull out of the bottom and not set again, or perhaps to foul, for example. Or if the boat's swinging room has to be restricted. In such cases, two anchors may well be better than one – and sometimes, although rarely, even three may be better than two.

There are two major methods of increasing security and using two anchors: breasting, and bow-and-stern anchoring.

BREASTING

When two anchors lead out in opposite directions from the bow, a boat is said to be *breasted* between two anchors. The technique for breasting is as follows:

(1) The boat is run toward the direction of primary wind or current. Approximately three boatlengths from the position the skipper wishes the boat to come to rest, the first anchor is dropped and its rode paid out freely.

(2) The boat is allowed to continue past its eventual position until it is approximately four boatlengths beyond the first anchor.

(3) A that point, strain is taken on the first rode, and the boat's motion is slowed as the first anchor is set. The boat is permitted to continue forward, while it is also turned so the stern swings slightly away from the first rode passing aft.

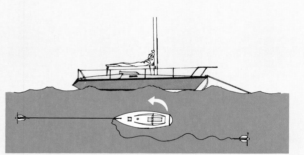

Two anchors are necessary where space is restricted such as an estuary, or where a tide change is expected that will swing the boat through 180°.

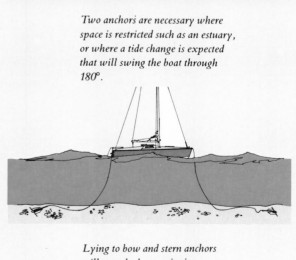

Lying to bow and stern anchors will stop the boat swinging to the tide or wind.

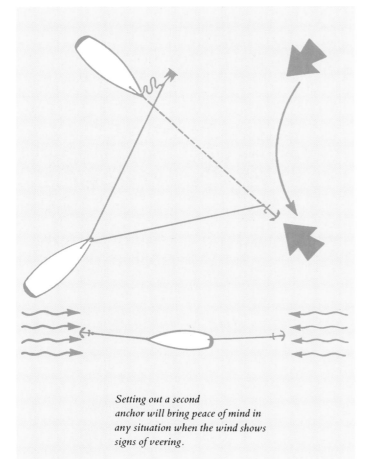

*Setting out a second
anchor will bring peace of mind in
any situation when the wind shows
signs of veering.*

between both rodes, always keeping her bow toward wind or current. In bow-and-stern anchoring, each end is alternately presented to the wind or current.

Both breasting and bow-and-stern anchoring can be accomplished in other ways. A good alternative is to anchor in the primary direction first, and then take a second anchor out in the dinghy to its proper position. Strain can be taken and the second hook set with some maneuvering. Here's where a good heavy kedge can be worth its weight in gold, as it can simply be taken out and dropped, with just a few tugs required to get it set.

Anchoring may seem complex, but if it is done right it will produce a feeling of self-sufficiency quite unlike that produced by any other endeavor. When coupled with a lovely harbor, a pretty sunset, good companionship, and a hot meal, the reasons for cruising at all become absolutely clear.

If the tide turns or the wind swings through 180° you might find two anchors get into a tangle. One way to avoid this is to set the first one, then pay out twice the length of the cable you need before dropping the second one. Next, take up half the length of the first rode until the boat lies at the mid-point. Then shackle the chains together, or lash the ropes, and lower them so that they are below the level of the keel. This way you have created a swivel about which the boat can turn.

(4) The first anchor bites, and forward motion is stopped just as the boat reaches a point three boatlengths past its intended position – six boatlengths past the first anchor.

(5) The second anchor is dropped, with the boat ready to back away from it. The engine is reversed, and the boat is backed away from the second anchor in a direction toward the first, but with its stern well clear of the first's rode. Slack in the first rode is taken up slowly as the boat backs.

(6) The second anchor is set normally, and the boat positioned between the two anchors.

BOW AND STERN

Bow-and-stern anchoring is done in precisely the same manner as breasting, with the exception that the first anchor may be set off the stern, and its rode controlled so as to keep it completely clear of the propeller.

In bow-and-stern anchoring, the stern rode is made fast to a fitting at the transom, and the boat is kept in line between the two anchors.

Note that in breasting, the boat is allowed to swing

*Anchoring provides an opportunity
to enjoy varied and splendid scenery,
which is such an important part of
the pleasure of sailing.*

A Caribbean anchorage.

ANCHORING PROBLEMS

There may come a time when a squall or a tidal change or a drastic change in wind direction causes an anchor to break its hold on the bottom. When this happens, there are several things to do.

DRAGGING

(1) First, you needn't worry about sleeping through a dragging, when something changes in the middle of the night. If a squall blows through, the noise and commotion is enough to wake you; and if a wind shift takes you around and starts moving you down the anchorage, the boat's motion should change enough to get your attention. Of course, if you sleep through all that, the sound when you bounce off the next boat is sure to wake you.

(2) Second, you should keep calm. Stand at the bow and either take bearings of fixed objects on the shore or line them up in a transit. A change in the bearing or transit indicates the boat is moving. Some modern electronic aids such as depth sounders and position indicators have alarms which can prove helpful. Best of all though are your natural senses. Sailors develop a feel for a sound or some such clue which indicates the boat is dragging. If you have any doubts, stand an anchor watch or at least take a look out of the hatch a number of times during the night. Examine your landmarks (anchor bearings) and determine how far you've gone and how fast you're dragging. Wake your crew calmly, and instruct them to dress quickly.

(3) Get yourself into the cockpit and start the engine, first making sure there are no stray lines in the water to foul the propeller. Determine where the anchor is right now. It may be under the boat or dead astern, in which case, you might be able to get clear and turn her by pushing the helm over. It's usually best to give the helm

a push to leeward; you might be able to get her to round up into the wind. However, and luckily, most boats tend to drag anchor with the bow slightly towards the wind, so it may be possible to maneuver with the engine.

(4) Shift to reverse once you've determined where the anchor is. Get someone forward immediately to handle the rode. Once the boat is backing, try to slip more scope and get the anchor to set. If other boats are too close, see the next step.

(5) Shift to forward and get the bow pointed to windward. Instruct the bowman to haul on the rode until the boat's bow is directly over the anchor. Haul in the anchor until it is clear of the water and dangling, ready to drop again.

(6) Power to a new spot in the clear, making sure you adhere to the original criteria for finding a spot. Drop anchor and go through the normal procedure for setting.

This small cruiser, left at anchor in a gentle offshore breeze, is now in danger from an onshore breeze and *breaking waves which are puting a great strain on its ground tackle.*

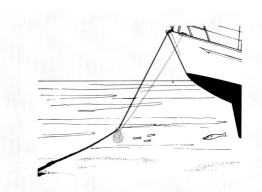

A weight or sack of weights let down the anchor rode on a messenger line *allows you to shorten scope in overcrowded anchorages.*

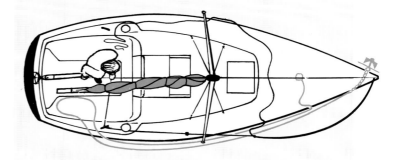

Singlehanders would be well advised to consider this arrangement for anchoring from the cockpit. Make *sure all lines are led outside the lifelines.*

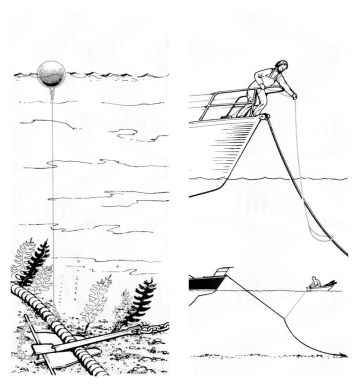

*(MIDDLE LEFT) A trip line,
buoyed at the surface,
can be a godsend when confronted
with a fouled anchor.*

*(LEFT) Messengers can be used to
clear a fouled anchor or tangled*

Note that before a storm it is wise to let out more
rode than is usual. If an anchor turns in a windshift, or if
the wind becomes too much for its holding power, more
scope should enable it to dig in again of its own accord.

Also note that a Danforth is more prone to turning out
in a strong wind shift – especially one of more than 90°. A
CQR, on the other hand, is better in drastic shifts, as is a
yachtsman.

FOULING

There are times when you will foul the anchor, either on
sea-bed refuse or underwater cables or with another
anchor. First, try hauling in rode until it is vertically
aligned. Then move weight aft to try breaking it out or
supply appropriate leverage via a windlass. If this doesn't
work, try sailing or motoring out, pulling in the opposite
direction from which the anchor was originally set. So
much for the easy methods. All the rest take a certain
amount of real and imaginary labor. You can run a
loop of line or chain down over the anchor rode, carry
it out in the dinghy and then haul from the opposite
direction. Or you can use a grapnel (or a small hook as
such) from the *anchored* dinghy or try to pick up the
main anchor, or any obstructing cable. If the anchor and
rode are fouled by another boat's ground tackle, attempt
to raise both anchor *and* rode, securing it by a line to the
boat as you lift the pair higher and higher. Then try to
free the anchor by hand from the dinghy (secured to the
mother ship).

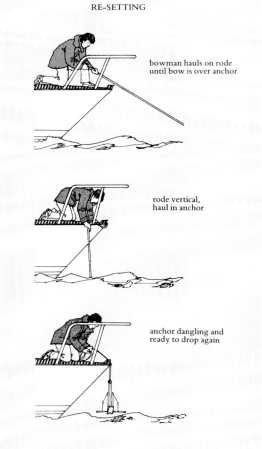

RE-SETTING

bowman hauls on rode
until bow is over anchor

rode vertical,
haul in anchor

anchor dangling and
ready to drop again

MOORING AND DOCKING

The problem of where to keep a boat faces every boatowner but a lot depends on the type of boat, the availability of moorings and the frequency of use.

BERTHS AND MARINAS

The vast increase in the popularity of boating has made finding a place to keep your boat difficult. Rivers which had free, swinging moorings 25 years ago will probably now have well-developed marinas if they are in popular sailing areas or are close to towns or cities. The difference in annual berthing charges is likely to be great although marinas offer convenience and a wider range of services.

For many people, the marina is the most convenient place in which to keep a boat. They are generally built in sheltered water such as harbors and rivers and they offer walk-on-board convenience. Sailing gear and provisions can be wheeled right alongside the boat.

There are many other benefits too, not least of which is some sort of security. This covers everything from having staff to make secure a chafed-through line, to 24-hour vigilance against theft of the boat or removable gear such as liferafts.

A good marina may also have water, electricity and telephone supplied for each berth; a chandlery and shop; a mobile hoist and crane for lifting boats and spars; a repair yard; a water and fuel berth; toilet and showers; a launderette; a transportation service linked with the local sail loft, and in the more recent developments, a bar, restaurant, boutique and even apartments and villas.

The berths themselves may be full length or just short finger pontoons to permit a greater density of boats. In either case, securing the boat and guarding against chafe is important. Instead of belaying the mooring warps directly to cleats or fairleads, some berth owners attach a short length of chain so that warps clear the pontoon edge. At the other end, attached to the boat, good fairleads are vital. They should have a soft radiused section free of any edges. If there is any edge at all it will do surprising damage to unprotected rope because a boat never stays still. Even when made fast, a boat will always be on the move. Some owners make up special fixed dock lines, shackled at one end to the pontoon, covered with anti-chafe PVC tubing where they lie across the boat and with a loop or bite spliced into the free end ready to slip over the yacht's own cleats.

Fenders are vital to protect the topsides from marking but they should hang at the correct height. It is common practice to suspend them from the life lines but this puts undue strain on them and it is better to use stanchion bases or specially fitted eyebolts. Owners anxious to preserve their topsides' finish will suspend a soft canvas sheet between the hull and the fenders and add extra fenders to the head and edges of the pontoon. If the yacht is particularly beamy amidships, it could pay to invest in two large spherical fenders to place either side of the widest point with ordinary fenders in between.

Even boats with relatively straight sides and a narrow beam are awkward shapes to tie up. Obviously bow and stern have to be secured; lines that lead forward and aft from the boat to the shore are called head (or bow) and stern lines. Those that lead at right angles to the boat are known as breast ropes but they do little to stop the boat surging backwards and forwards – so springs have to be used too. One leads aft from a point between

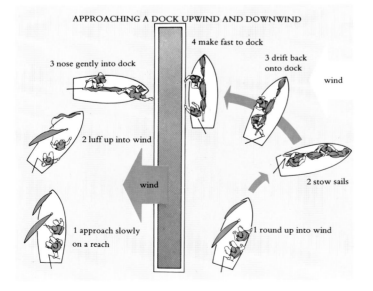

APPROACHING A DOCK UPWIND AND DOWNWIND

4 make fast to dock

3 nose gently into dock

3 drift back onto dock

wind

2 luff up into wind

2 stow sails

wind

1 approach slowly on a reach

1 round up into wind

A Typical marina (ABOVE).

The nomenclature and positioning of lines (RIGHT).

The correct way to approach a dock (BOTTOM LEFT), depending on wind direction. If in doubt, drop all sail and row or paddle in.

bow line

back spring

Dock

fore spring

stern line

the bow and amidships to the shore (bow or fore spring), and another forward from between the stern and amidships to the shore (stern or back spring).

In general the springs should be taut with the breast, bow and stern lines a little slack. If the berth is in a tidal river and the springs are attached as above, (instead of both sharing one cleat amidships), it should be possible to adjust the lines so that the water flow lifts the boat slightly away from the pontoon – a much better arrangement than being pinned hard on to it.

Making fast alongside a dock, pontoon or jetty is probably the most common boat handling situation a skipper is likely to face.

Approaches under power are preferable. If the wind and tide are parallel to the shore make your approach into the stronger to ensure maximum control.

If the wind is onshore you can slow and stop the boat just off the dock and be blown, even into very tight spaces, by letting the wind drift the boat in. In an offshore breeze, steer in at a more acute angle, straightening up at the last moment and making sure both bow and stern lines are made fast quickly.

When approaching under sail, look for the largest gap to give yourself more room to slow and stop the boat. Use a mainsail-only approach if the wind is blowing off the dock, when both wind and tide are running parallel to the quay or if a fresh wind is blowing in the opposite direction to the tide.

Headsail-only approaches can be attempted when there is an onshore wind or a fast tide running against a gentle wind.

Control of speed is everything in such maneuvers. Make sure the mainsail can be eased right out if necessary or the jib half lowered or even dropped completely if you need to burn off speed.

Because berthing density is so great in a marina, some operators insist that boats enter and leave only under power. Because space is so tight the simple marina berth may require quite complex maneuvers, especially if your boat does not handle well astern, or if there is no space to turn normally.

Strong winds or fast running tides cause the majority of problems in marinas, preventing the boat from turning fast enough or pinning it against the pontoon.

In most circumstances it should be possible to turn into the berth and have the crew step neatly ashore with the lines. If the wind or tide is taking the boat away from the berth, steer at it, and straighten her up at the last moment. When leaving, a gentle push off the pontoon and a burst of power should do the trick.

If, when you want to leave, the wind or tide is pinning the boat against the pontoon, it is likely that the bow won't swing sufficiently toward wind or tide for the boat to turn. In these circumstances, slip all the lines

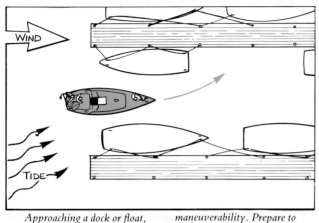

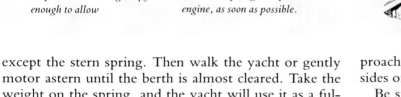

Approaching a dock or float, precautions must be made to keep the boat moving only fast enough to allow *maneuverability. Prepare to stop the boat, either through lines to the pilings or by engine, as soon as possible.*

When tied up to a dock with an onshore wind (LEFT), an anchor set outboard from the far side of the boat will prevent damage caused by the ship banging against the pier wall.

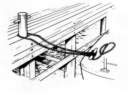

Endless-loop mooring lines allow a singlehander to cast off from the helm without dockside assistance.

except the stern spring. Then walk the yacht or gently motor astern until the berth is almost cleared. Take the weight on the spring, and the yacht will use it as a fulcrum. But watch the bows: they will swing in a wide arc and might not clear the opposite pontoon or neighbouring yacht, without the spring being used again.

Alternatively, just keeping the bow line tight after the others have been cast off may be enough to swing the yacht off the berth and for her to motor clear of all the potential obstacles.

If you have a regular berth, arrange permanent dock lines attached to the piles which can be hung on a hook on each pile. Then, you should be able to simply reach out for them at a convenient height, rather than fish for them in the water with a boat hook.

When a cross-wind or tide is present, be sure to allow for drift and aim to secure the uptide/upwind warps first. Similarly, when leaving, these lines should be last to be slipped.

Often the pier will be quite high; be prepared to scale the wall (hope there is a ladder) with both bow *and* stern lines in hand. Spring lines can be rigged after bow and stern are secured. Should the ship be tied up on the windward side of the dock, a kedge can be run out to hold it off, either from a spring cleat amidships or with two warps leading from the kedge to both bow and stern cleats.

You may suddenly have to change your intended approach or goal because of either the unexpected appearance of a smaller, hitherto unseen, boat or directions from the dockmaster. Lines, fenders, etc. will have to be quickly switched. If you have enough time, it pays to back off and reapproach *after* these chores have been completed. If not, and the area is crowded on first ap-

proach, it is a good idea to rig lines and fenders on both sides of the boat.

Be sure in any tidal area that enough slack is kept in the docking line to allow for the rise and fall of the ship. A good idea is to lead the lines to the dock pilings or cleats in a bight and then back again to the deck cleats. In this manner, you will be able to make adjustments without leaving the deck.

Should the berth be one that dries out at low tide, attempt to heel the boat slightly inward toward the dock. A line passed about the mast at spreader height and led ashore will usually do the trick. Be careful that the rigging does not come in contact with the dock, and that the spreaders will not be damaged. A block attached to a halyard and also held around the mast with a strap or loose loop of rope can be hoisted aloft to just below the spreaders *after* a line from the dock has been led through it and back to the dock or to a cleat on deck. In addition, a heavy anchor can be placed on the dockside of the vessel.

BEACHING

As you approach a beach, prepare to do two things: get the centerboard or daggerboard up, and get the rudder's blade up. A centerboard will normally ride up by itself when it strikes the bottom, making it a fine tool for sounding the depth as you're sailing in toward your beach (although this is inadvisable with a rocky bottom, which could damage the board). Raising a daggerboard is trickier.

With a daggerboard, raise it in stages. As the bottom approaches, pull it halfway out of its trunk. Then, as you feel bottom, lift it right out and stow it in the boat.

SOME POINTS TO CONSIDER WHEN DOCKING

Approaching any dock or pier or pontoon is made more difficult by the tight quarters, proximity of other vessels and the tricks tidal streams can play around pilings and walls. Make due allowance for windage, drift and lost control at low speeds. Know how your boat handles! Attempt to approach to windward. With wind and tide behind you, you will have to either play with bursts of reverse on the throttle or have a crew member stationed to drop a stern anchor to slow down the ship and allow for some control.

(BELOW) Rafting up in a crowded marina.

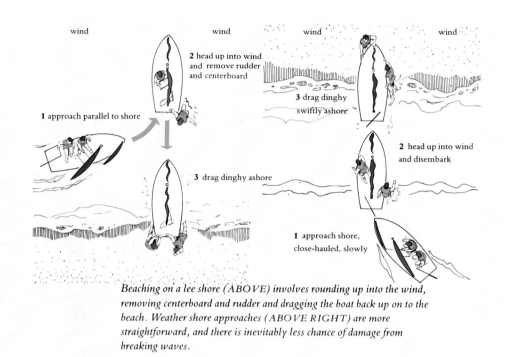

Beaching on a lee shore (ABOVE) involves rounding up into the wind, removing centerboard and rudder and dragging the boat back up on to the beach. Weather shore approaches (ABOVE RIGHT) are more straightforward, and there is inevitably less chance of damage from breaking waves.

wind

1 approach parallel to shore

2 head up into wind and remove rudder and centerboard

3 drag dinghy ashore

3 drag dinghy swiftly ashore

2 head up into wind and disembark

1 approach shore, close-hauled, slowly

Once you're feeling the bottom, either with dagger-board or centerboard, let the sails luff, allowing the sheet to run free to spill the wind completely out of the sail, and step gently out of the boat. Get around astern and dismount (or *unship*) the rudder and position the boat directly into the wind if she isn't pointed that way.

Always try to pick a windward shore for a beaching, for the land shields the water from the wind, keeping wave-action to a minimum. Any waves present will be easier to handle than big breaking waves.

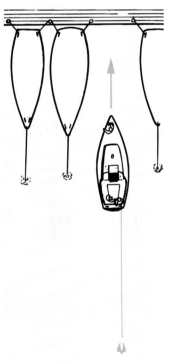

Mediterranean moors are usually stern-to. Try entering bow on, as this will give you much greater control over the boat, especially when alone.

PILE MOORINGS

Can be an intermediate step between marinas and swinging moorings. They permit far more boats to be moored in a given area than on the swinging variety but they do not give a marina's walk-on convenience. Piles with metal bars attached to them are driven into the sea or river bed. Running up and down these bars are rings to which the mooring lines are attached. As a boat rises and falls with the tide, so the lines slide the rings up and down. Often two boats lie between each set of piles and if they moor bow to stern their masts should be well clear of each other in case wash from a passing vessel causes them to rock together. However, other factors may override this, such as the preferred uptide approach or the wind strength.

Unless there is no alternative, pile moorings are best tackled under power rather than sail. Again, assess whether wind or tide is strongest and plan an approach in the relevant direction. The aim with pile moorings is to attach both a bow line and a stern line.

If the wind and tide are from the same direction you should be able to nose the bow toward the upwind/uptide pile so that the bow line can be attached. Then you can drop back, secure the stern line and adjust both lines until the boat is equidistant between the two.

When wind and tide are opposed, steer into the stronger of the two and attach the stern line first. Then it should be paid out as the boat moves forward, to attach the bow line. This is known as a running moor because you secure the line as you pass the pile. Clearly, the line must be tended throughout the moor to stop it fouling the propeller.

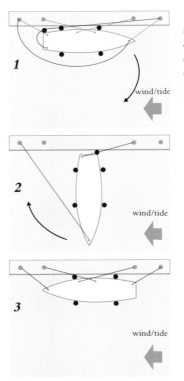

Warping the boat round. 1 Rig two new lines: one from the bow around the outside, across the stern and to the shore, and the other around the stern, inside the boat to the shore. 2 All other lines are released. Let the wind or tide push the boat around. Fendering must be effective. 3 Rig the mooring lines as normal when alongside again.

The same system is used if the wind and tide are at right-angles. Invariably the wind will be on the beam and the piles are laid in line with the tide, so after attaching the stern line, steer upwind to attach the bow line.

Because control of the boat is so vital, attempting this under sail is not recommended. It could be better to consider other options. You might try just treating one pile as a mooring and thus make sure of getting a bow line secure. Then take a stern line out to the other pile

When a second boat approaches a pile mooring, one method is to make fast to the existing boat. A bow line can then be taken forward by a tender.

Rafting up (FAR TOP RIGHT): fenders must be adjusted to a suitable height.

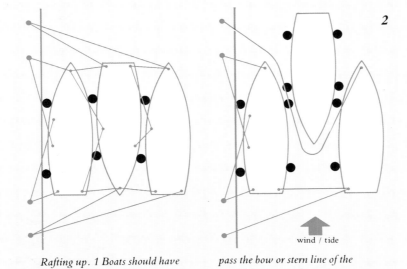

1

2

wind / tide

Rafting up. 1 Boats should have bow, stern and spring lines as normal. 2 When leaving a raft slip out gently downwind/downtide;

pass the bow or stern line of the outside boat around your bow so that her crew can close up the raft.

with the tender. Or if another boat is lying between the piles, go in alongside her and rig your lines as quickly as possible to ensure the other boat's lines are not unduly overstrained.

To leave pile moorings you will need to double up your lines so that they can be slipped. This means passing them through the ring and bringing the bitter-end back on board. The benefit of two really long lines will become obvious as joined lines will not run through the ring easily. When you are ready to go, slip the line under the least load first so that the remaining line keeps the boat facing into the wind and tide.

If you are alongside another boat, the bow and stern lines can be recovered by the tender and then you can depart normally.

Instead of piles, some harbors or rivers might have fore-and-aft buoys and they can be tackled the same way.

RAFTING UP

If you are sailing in company, or visiting a popular harbor, it is most likely you will have to raft up.

Be sure to ask permission of the vessel you wish to go alongside and arrange your fenders at a suitable height. You will need the usual complement of bow, stern and spring lines. In addition you will need lines long enough to run from your bow and stern to the shore, otherwise the raft will move around too much.

Because of the shape of boats, it can help to lie in the opposite direction to your neighbor. This will help the

boats mesh together better, keep their masts apart and allow some privacy in the cockpit.

Ask when other boats in the raft wish to leave, as extricating one boat from the middle is not easy. If necessary the boat outside the departing vessel may have to let go her bow line, pass it behind, and outside, of her inside neighbor and secure it to the shore. As the departing vessel slips out, the outside vessel pulls in on her shore line to close the gap, before making fast in the normal way to her new inside neighbor.

WARPING A BOAT AROUND

There may be occasions when you wish to turn the boat around, perhaps so that you can depart in a more favorable direction, or you might be moored at the head of an enclosed basin and not have enough room to turn once under way. The choice of whether to pivot around on the bow or stern will, as ever, depend on the wind or tide. You will find it difficult to swing against whichever is the strongest. But using these natural forces can make for an elegant and easy solution.

You will need extra fenders around which the boat will turn. Then, if you are to pivot on the stern and swing the bow around, rig a new line from the outside of the bow to lead aft around the stern, and back to the pier. Likewise rig a line on the outside of the stern quarter, around the transom and forward inside the boat and dock. Release all other lines and use these two to turn the boat around.

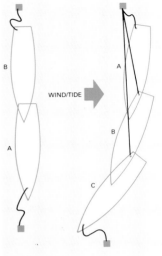

Pile moorings. Attach the bow line first (ABOVE), then drop to secure the stern before adjusting lines to bring the boat to mid-point between the piles. With wind and/or tide abeam attach the stern line first. Then motor forward into the wind or tide to attach the bow line before centralizing the boat. A pontoon mooring (LEFT), showing fenders and dock lines.

BUOY MOORINGS

To many sailors, a boat nodding gently at her mooring buoy in an idyllic setting epitomizes the attraction and freedom of boat ownership. However, swinging moorings have their own problems. They are often laid in an open roadstead subject to high winds and rough seas, or in a small harbor with fishing boat or ferry traffic, or in an area with only enough water to float keel boats at high water.

In the latter case a bilge keel or lifting keel arrangement is necessary, although fin keelers with drying-out legs rigged on either side may also take the bottom. All boats need a decent bow roller. The requirements here are high cheeks, a secure 'keep' pin and fittings of stout enough construction and attachment to take the load of a boat surging up and down in rough weather or lying across the wind or tide.

Backing this up should be a samson post. The advantage of such a fitting, as opposed to a cleat, is that chain can be made fast to it in such a way that it can be released under load. Take two turns around the post or bollard and then pass a loop underneath the taut chain and slip it over the post.

Moored bows-to (ABOVE). With no significant wind or tide and plenty of space available, maneuvering in or out should present little difficulty under power.

A modern 28-footer (8.5m), with a fractional sloop rig (ABOVE).

The problem of making chain fast can be simplified by having a ready-made loop in the end which can be passed over a cleat or post. Usually the mooring pick-up buoy will have a short length of rope between the buoy and the chain and this can be made up over the loop to make it doubly secure.

The pick-up buoy should be marked with the boat's name and, if you are happy to allow visitors to use your mooring when you are away, the weight of boat the mooring will safely hold and your intended period of absence.

A useful addition is a second smaller buoy attached to the main mooring buoy, weighted at the bottom and with a light pole protruding from the top which can be grabbed so that the mooring buoy can be brought alongside. Other tricks of the trade include using a patented boat hook which latches a line on to the buoy automatically and the padding of the chain with PVC tubing to prevent it damaging the boat's topsides when it rides over the mooring buoy at the turn of the tide.

All manner of objects have been used as weights on the sea-bed – old engine blocks, concrete-filled tires and old mill wheels. The important thing is that the weight, or anchor mooring, should be heavy enough for the boat and for local conditions. The chain attached to it should be of the correct diameter too. Just like the boat herself, the mooring will require regular inspection and maintenance. The chain should be galvanized and tested. Any shackles in the system should be wired up to prevent accidental loosening.

Moorings are usually under the control of a boat or harbor authority who control their laying and density.

LYING STERN-TO

Some marinas have boats lying stern-to rather than alongside a finger pontoon. Securing the bow will be either a pair of piles to which lines are attached or a mooring buoy attached to a ground chain or weight under water. If you use such a marina, you will find the step-through style of pulpit or stern boarding ladder arrangement of real benefit.

If there is no significant wind or tide the boat can be steered in either bow or stern first. Control the speed so that the crew can put a line over the pile or attach it to a ring on it. In the case of a mooring, the buoy will have to be picked up with a boat hook. Then motor toward the dock so that the shore lines from either side of a boat can be made fast; the weight of all lines pulling against each other will hold the boat clear of the dock.

If you lie stern-to it might help to cross the stern lines so that they act like springs. As a general rule, the more a line can act at an acute angle to the boat, the more it is able to hold it in a given position.

BASIC MOORING UNDER SAIL

As you approach your mooring, check on the wind direction in relation to the positions of the buoy and any nearby obstacles. Be aware of wind direction all the time, and trim properly for whatever point of sail you are on as you approach the mooring area.

The basic maneuver is to get downwind of the mooring buoy while keeping some speed on the boat, and then as you reach a point directly downwind of the buoy, round up quickly and coast directly upwind, sails luffing until you can reach out and take the buoy and make it fast.

Some things to keep in mind: when rounding up your boat you must be going slowly enough not to pass the mooring.

One way to kill speed is to let the sheet run out and luff the sail, even as you approach your rounding-up point. Another speed-killer is the rounding-up maneuver itself. The more drastic it is, the more speed it takes off.

If you round up and find that you cannot quite coast to the mooring, but are slowing to a stop a bit short, you can try sculling up to the buoy vigorously pushing the tiller from side to side.

In time, after some practice, you will learn how much room you need to perform this maneuver, and how to handle your boat as you approach on different points of sail and different wind conditions. But at first, if there's enough space, try to perform the maneuver from a reach. You will be able to see your path better, and your turning angles will be simplest.

Don't worry if you feel uncomfortable at first sailing to a mooring. Take all sail down in the clear and row or paddle to the mooring.

Swinging moorings

······· CHAPTER EIGHT ·······

A BIT OF A BLOW

The seaman knows the language of meteoro-
logy, how the elements affect the weather and
the limits of his own ability and those of his
yacht in dealing with those elements. The
technical terms involved are those that describe cloud
formations and atmospheric pressure systems as in
weather forecasts on radio and television and in the press.

THE CLOUDS

Clouds are excellent indicators of the weather. Generally
speaking, it is not looming black clouds which indicate
change but wispy and fibrous white/grey clouds. They
are often a portent of deteriorating conditions and the
faster they move the sooner the change can be expected.
CUMULUS CLOUDS Separate, flat-based and with little
vertical height, they usually denote fair weather.
STRATOCUMULUS These are dense and form large banks
giving rise to complete cloud cover.
STRATOS A low mist-like cloud which in fair conditions
can produce a sea fog.
NIMBOSTRATOS Rain-bearing clouds associated with
fronts and giving steady rain.
CUMULONIMBUS Deep shower and thunder clouds.
They mark unstable conditions and often have the
characteristic anvil head.

PRESSURE SYSTEMS

Areas of low pressure are known as cyclones or depressions. They occur when air rises from low levels to high
levels and is cooled. This causes both clouds and precipitation. High pressure areas, or anticyclones, have
descending air which warms as it falls, dispersing cloud
and inhibiting precipitation.

Weather maps are very similar to land relief maps
where, instead of the contours joining points of the
same height, they run between points with the same
barometric pressure.

'Lows' are shown on the weather chart as areas of low pressure surrounded by isobars with ascending air. A 'high' often has its rings of isobars spaced much further apart.

Due to the earth's rotation the wind blows counter-clockwise around a low and clockwise around a high in the northern hemisphere. The wind's path closely corresponds to the isobars and the closer their spacing the stronger the wind. In the southern hemisphere the directions are reversed, and close isobars of course still indicate strong wind.

LOW PRESSURE SYSTEMS Depressions are born when two different air masses meet. Then, air pressure drops as a cyclonic circulation occurs like a spiral winding itself up. A 'low' in the northern hemisphere will advance eastwards drawing in warm, subtropical air as it goes. The boundary of the warm air is marked by the warm front, while the cold air behind the cold front tries to overtake it. When the cold air finally overtakes the warm air and curls around it, the front is said to be occluded. Such fronts are characteristic of old and dying depressions.

HIGH PRESSURE SYSTEMS For continental Europe and certain coasts of North America and Australasia, high pressure can bring settled spells of weather. A slack pressure gradient allows winds to be created by other factors with temperature the most frequent cause. Sea breezes often blow in coastal areas, especially during spring and summer. Sea breezes are a consequence of the sun warming the land more than the water, causing the air above the land to expand and rise. The air above the sea is sucked in to fill the void.

A slack pressure gradient and convection aided by cumulus cloud helps the creation of sea breezes. Often these blow in mid to late afternoon, lasting until mid evening. The sea breeze may have to overcome an existing wind and there may be a pronounced wind shift, as much as 180°, as the new breeze establishes itself.

It is common for coasts to experience sea breezes by day and for a wind to blow from the land by night. This effect is most pronounced in temperate latitudes in spring and summer but sea breezes dominate tropical, and other, regions all year round.

Land breezes are caused by the reverse effect of a sea breeze. Because of this diurnal pattern boats on passage may find it easier to leave port and clear the coast in the early morning and arrive, with a good tail wind, in mid to late afternoon.

Another type of wind is the katabatic variety, which sinks under gravity and boosts the land breeze. Together with its opposite, anabatics which are upslope winds, these breezes produce puzzling and highly localized conditions. Anabatics blow on to slopes on sunny mornings, drawing air away from those slopes left in shadow. On their way up the slopes, they precipitate moisture. Once at the top, the cold, dense air spills over the peak and sinks down the other slope by gravity rather like a katabatic wind. This wind warms as it tumbles down due to increasing pressure and it rushes out over plains and the sea.

The point for sailors to note is that only a slight pressure gradient is needed for such winds as they gain their strength from temperature change caused by strong sun in hilly terrain. The Mistral, for instance, can exceed gale force, so it is a wind to be cautious of.

BAD WEATHER

Few sailors want to be caught out in heavy weather, although tough conditions to one might be enjoyable to another, depending on the size of their boat, their level of experience and whether they are sailing upwind or downwind. Beating into a 20 knot breeze blowing against a two-knot tide can be difficult enough. Remember that forecast wind strengths are averages, so it is possible to experience gusts up to 30 knots, even if a 20 knot was expected.

Preparation is the key. This can involve changing down sail sooner rather than later. It will help to have the next sail required stowed at the top of the locker or ready to hand below. It will also help to pre-cook hot food and have a supply of hot water or drink in a vacuum flask.

In planning your course you will need to allow for more leeway and to give yourself more sea room, particularly around headlands. Obviously, making sure that all hatches are secured, that the crew are properly clothed and wearing safety gear and that all loose gear is stowed is fundamental.

Avoiding bad weather is better than meeting it, so if you are able to reach shelter, do so. This will entail finding a place for which you have relevant charts, tide and approach information and making sure that you are not bringing the boat into greater danger than you would be by staying at sea.

Sailing in rough conditions is difficult. If you are beating upwind you will probably be sailing into the waves, although an increase in wind associated with the passage of a front can bring a sudden wind shift and consequently a confused sea. A passage upwind can be smoothed out by steering up the face of waves and bearing away on their crest, so that the boat slides down the

When sailing along the coast, it is usually possible to find shelter in a protected harbour before the weather has changed to affect the sea.

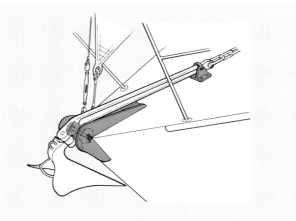

(ABOVE) Securing the main anchor at the ready is vital, especially with onshore winds and a shelving bottom. A CQR in a bow *roller with a drophead pin and a chock for the shank is certainly the most convenient way of going about it.*

(ABOVE) While running in severe conditions it will be necessary to slow the ship considerably. Trailing a bight of heavy line from the *quarters may be highly effective, especially as the length can be adjusted to coincide with the rhythm of the seas.*

(ABOVE) Lying ahull can be effective if the boat is not too deep-keeled and the windage aloft is balanced by reasonable underwater area. The idea is to keep the boat from tripping over into a roll while at the same time not being so stiff that rig or deck gear could be smashed.

(ABOVE) Heaving-to is not just a heavy weather tactic. It is especially useful for singlehanders who need a respite in bad weather or want to prepare a meal and cannot otherwise leave the helm. Modern fin-keel boats will not always heave-to with ease. Experiments with sail area and set may be needed.

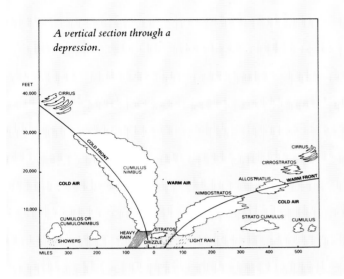

A vertical section through a depression.

back. This should reduce somewhat the spray thrown from the bow as you punch into the wave and make for a softer landing on its other side.

Steering downwind, the problem can be the boat travelling faster than the waves themselves. Modern lightweight racing hulls can surf down the face of waves at great speed with an expert crew pushing the boat hard under lots of sail. With less sail set however, the boat can be picked up by one wave, stopped in the back of the next and then find her stern swung round by the following wave.

There are various techniques for dealing with heavy weather. Most require room to drift to leeward and there are no hard and fast rules as to which suits a particular type of boat. When beating or reaching you may heave-to to ride out rough weather. This entails backing the jib (perhaps by tacking and not releasing the jib sheet) and tying the helm to leeward. The mainsail is then trimmed so that the boat lies steadily with the bows pointing slightly upwind.

If the waves are large there could be a danger of their breaking on to the sails and putting undue strain on the rig. To avoid this you can lie ahull. The sails are dropped, securely stowed, the helm lashed to leeward and the boat left to ride out the foul weather.

The motion may be too violent to make lying ahull tenable for long, in which case you may wish to run off downwind, although this will require a guiding hand on the helm. To slow the boat down and to give the helm something to bite against, it is possible either to stream a line or a drogue. However, for either to be really effective they need to be long enough to stream two waves behind the boat. Good fairleads and cleats are essential and to stand any chance of recovering, the line or drogue will need to be led to the most powerful winch.

PREPARING FOR A SQUALL

The best way to handle a squall is to know when to expect it, and to head for cover before it hits. Tracking the storm visually is the best way to know whether it's going to pass through your area, and augmenting your own observations with those of local radio broadcasts can create a reasonably good picture of the expected pattern of weather.

If you're too far from land to take cover, and the storm is headed your way, however, you must be prepared.

Expect a short period of turbulent weather, with winds possibly as strong as 60–80 mph, hard pelting rain, some possible hail, and lightning. Secure all loose gear topside and below. Close all belowdecks openings – ports, hatches.

Even if your boat is adequately grounded against lightning strike, suspend a length of chain from the amidships shrouds into the water, taping the contact point. Make sure to connect the chain to the masthead (upper) shroud.

As the squall approaches, check that no lines are in the water, switch on engine and douse all sail and furl it securely. Do this far enough in advance to allow plenty of time to get yourself and your crew settled.

Break out the foul-weather gear, and unpack the lifejackets and make sure each crewman knows he's got one. Run through a quick fire-safety drill, making sure everyone knows where the extinguishers are and how to use them. Turn off your radio telephone and disconnect its antenna.

With the engine running at about half-speed, point the bow directly into the squall cloud as it approaches. Send everyone else below. If there is moderate vessel traffic about, the helmsman must remain topside. If there is heavy traffic, one lookout should also remain on deck. Any crew topside should wear safety harness.

As the wind hits, make sure the vessel has steerageway against it. More throttle may be needed.

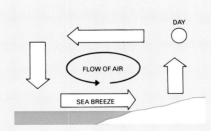

The flow of air which creates a sea breeze. As air rises from the land warmed by the sun, cooler air is drawn in off the sea. This in turn is warmed, rises, cools as it gains height and falls again over the sea.

Several lines can be joined to form a loop so that the load can be spread from either quarter although a bridle will achieve the same effect. Recent research on drogues has shown that a cat's-cradle of light line across the neck of the drogue will stop it tangling up as it is rotated in the breaking crest of a wave. Such drogues can even be of help in moderate conditions to control the stern when crossing a bar guarding a harbor entrance.

When running away from the wind, some sail can be carried if there is sufficient room. A storm jib for instance, sheeted in hard on the centerline may help by holding the stern to the wind and seas.

SOME POINTS TO CONSIDER IN HEAVYWEATHER

When the weather deteriorates to a point where handling ship under reduced sail becomes difficult, when the size of the seas endangers the integrity of the ship, or when progress in a safe direction becomes near impossible, you are in danger.

Everything on deck *and* below must be secured in heavy weather. Sails, anchors, lines, liferaft, you must be attached to the boat in a manner that precludes loss overboard. You must be in a life harness.

Safety harnesses are *de rigeur* at night and in anything over 18 knots. They ought to be well built with two lanyards with strong hooks/snaps. Deck attachment points must be through-bolted.

Trailing lines does work. However, they must be many and attached so as to distribute the strains around the ship. Occasionally, anchors can be trailed from lines or bundles of chain.

In 'survival conditions' – force 10 and upward – the only possible point of sail will be running. In fact, because of the strength of the wind and the severity and height of the seas, you will run no matter what. In such circumstances, it is best to rid the decks of any and all impedimenta that may be carried away or hamper such working of the deck as is possible.

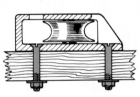

All deck fittings must be through-bolted with backing plates. The strains imposed in heavy-weather sailing can otherwise rip even the most robust hardware from its position.

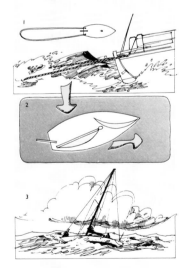

Classic techniques for weathering or riding out a gale. Streaming a long loop of rope astern (1). Hove-to with jib backed (2). Lying ahull with all sail stowed (3).

The helmsman must concentrate hard as a crest rises astern. Note the safety harness line clipped to a secure point.

Heavily reinforced storm sails (RIGHT) – jib and trysail instead of mainsail – enable a boat to keep sailing in all but the severest weather and claw off dangerous lee shores.

With proper storm canvas or well-reefed sails (LEFT) it should be possible to beat off a lee shore in a gale. This assumes a weatherly hull and the skills to use these sail combinations successfully. Practice in moderate weather will familiarize you with the limitations of shortened canvas.

HEAVY WEATHER OFFSHORE

Battening down Ports and hatches should be closed and secured whenever there is danger of seas breaking around or over the boat's decks.

Bearing off Just as in an inshore blow, it is wise not to struggle to windward in a big sea offshore. Let her fall off to a broad reach or run and ease her motion, and remember to mind the helm against broaching. Reaching broadside to a really big sea is not a good idea, as a breaking crest could knock the boat down, and water could come aboard.

Slowing her down Ocean waves whipped up by strong winds get far larger than those described thus far.

The first way to do this is to reduce sail. Hank on the smallest working jib, and reef the main as far as necessary. When that is still too much sail, secure all plain sail and rig the storm sails. Trim the storm sails to handle your offwind point of sail, just as you'd handle main and jib.

Even slower If the waves and wind are still driving the boat too fast and there is a danger of broaching, stream some gear astern to act as a brake.

Lying ahull If there just isn't quite enough sea room to keep running off in a gale, whether streaming lines or not, then a boat must be stopped at sea. One way to do this is to lie ahull – which simply means that all sail is taken off, the hatches are battened and the boat is left to her own devices. Sometimes, a skipper will want to experiment with lashing the tiller or wheel in several positions until he finds one that will steer the boat into an optimum attitude against wind and sea.

Heaving-to If lying ahull still creates too much drift, and there isn't enough sea room, then heaving-to may be the answer. Heaving-to is stopping her with her bow headed into the wind and sea, and requires either storm sails or *sea anchor.*

HEAVY WEATHER INSHORE

The best technique in windward sailing in a rough inshore chop is to bear off a little, keeping the seas off the bow to present more of the boat's side to the waves.

The surface of the sea usually has a pattern – a repeating cycle, a rhythm. Larger waves come in groups, followed by periods of relatively smaller seas when you can work the boat more to windward, bearing off only when those seas too big to breast come rolling down.

In restricted waters inshore, a rough sea can be problematic for a number of reasons:

(1) You could get caught off a *lee shore.* This is when the wind and sea overcome a boat and drive her towards a land mass. Always have an alternative course of action planned to avoid a lee shore. If there is no safe harbor to leeward, reach off some distance to get into the clear and ride it out.

(2) Maneuverability is greatly reduced in heavy seas. Traffic and/or obstructions may be hard to avoid.

(3) Your crew's effectiveness may be greatly impaired. Seasickness is often unavoidable, despite a number of new treatments.

The most prudent course of action in an inshore blow is to seek shelter as soon as you find the conditions uncomfortable. The best technique is to alter course off the wind, taking the seas on your quarter as on a broad reach, and head for the nearest harbor in that direction – even if it means not making your destination that day.

FOG

Reduced visibility is of great concern to the small craft navigator. Fog and mist are one and the same thing, namely visibility obscured by water droplets in the air, with fog being the thicker of the two. Haze is due to solid particles.

Fog is caused by the surface temperature being colder than the air mass above it and so condensing the water vapor.

Fog found at sea is often advection fog, ie a transfer of conditions in a horizontal, as opposed to a vertical, plane of convection. Fog conditions occur as the air leaves the land; fog is therefore rarely found on windward coasts. The incidence of fog is also more likely with low wind speeds. Higher wind speeds cause fog to lift and form low stratus cloud.

Radiation fog may also affect waters surrounded largely by land. Land cools rapidly at night and the warm air rises and the land surface becomes chilled. Dawn is the worst time and this type of fog is most prevalent from autumn to spring.

Cold rising ocean currents are another cause of fog, the Grand Banks of Newfoundland being the area most famous for this.

In fog, your position soon becomes doubtful, even though you've been keeping track on your chart, so it's important to know the tides and currents and the times of high and low water in the area you're cruising. It's also important to know where the best harbour of refuge is. Even in known waters, the visibility can be so poor that you'll find yourself faced with several choices: *(1)* Anchor until the fog clears. Proper fog signals must be sounded regularly and clearly. *(2)* Turn around and steer a reciprocal course in the hope of sailing back out into the clear. *(3)* Hold your course, but slow down by reducing sail, and keep sounding your fog signals. Try to keep track of your speed and course so as to keep a running estimate on your position. If you're in open

SOME POINTS TO CONSIDER WHEN CAUGHT IN FOG

Fog is usually accompanied by little or no wind. However, there are times and places where dense fog will coexist with strong breezes. In such situations, decrease throttle if under power or reduce sail more than you would normally. In dense fogs, visibility may be down to less than 300 feet (90 metres), and anything other than dead slow ahead poses a real threat to the vessel and crew.

Human senses become less reliable in foggy conditons: sounds are distorted, shapes appear and disappear, ships creep in and out of banks that suddenly close in. The only reliable navigational tool in such situations is the traditional ship's compass. TRUST IT! No matter what your senses indicate, the compass is a safer bet. It is not subject to psychological pressures, it doesn't drink, and it won't fall overboard.

Fog signals: One blast: I am turning to starboard. Two blasts: I am turning to port.
Three blasts: I am going astern.
Five blasts: Beware! I am in doubt concerning your intentions.
Short, long, short blasts: Warning! Danger of collision.
These are to be sounded on a horn or whistle. The ringing of a bell signifies a vessel aground or at anchor.

Proceed with utmost caution.

The brute force of the sea (ABOVE) demands a healthy respect from all who venture out on it.

In lightning emergencies, a length of chain shackled to a chainplate or rigging screw (RIGHT) can partially substitute for proper internal grounding. Be sure the chain is long enough to stay in the water no matter how violently the ship may roll.

Thunder clouds forming indicate the risk of squalls (BOTTOM LEFT). The wisest course of action is to seek the closest upwind shelter.

Lightning protection should be arranged so that all shrouds, mast, stays, and rails are tied to a common ground (BELOW RIGHT).

water, this might be the best procedure of all.

It is wise to carry aboard a radar-reflective shape to hoist aloft in case of reduced visibility. Commercial vessels all have radar, and such a shape could enhance your visibility in traffic lanes, but, keep a vigilant look-out at all times.

THUNDER AND LIGHTNING

The earth, rather like a domestic electricity system, has its own flow of electricity – between the surface and the atmosphere. Thunderstorms are discharges to equalize that flow.

In tropical areas, thunderstorms occur with great frequency while in temperate latitudes they may be caused by an unstable airmass or be the precursor to a front. Whatever the cause, thunderstorms are marked by the sudden upward rush of warm, moist air reaching great heights. Unstable air masses will be charged unevenly electrically and equalization is needed. Lightning is the discharge which re-establishes an electrical equilibrium. An observer at sea can easily judge how far away a storm is. Sound at sea level travels at 720 mph (1150 km/h), so a five-second gap between a lightning flash and a thunderclap means that the storm is a mile (1.6 km) away.

There is a marked effect on the wind in such storms because the unstable airmass feeds on air drawn in at the bottom which is later dissipated in the storm itself. If the storm formation is to windward of your position, the air being sucked into the base will cancel out the prevailing wind so producing the lull before the storm. As it builds, winds will rush in from the direction of the storm. With the storm downwind of your position the suction effect increases the prevailing wind prior to the calm and then the storm itself. Such storms are usually a summer phenomenon and rarely last more than an hour. They should hold little threat for a boat because they give ample warning of the possible need to reduce sail.

Lightning strikes are rare and if your boat has its rig grounded to the keel bolts and hull fittings such a strike should do no more than knock out the electrical instruments.

One type of thunderstorm however may be more severe than others. This is the single cell storm which can grow against a strong prevailing wind. If thunder is heard in near gale force winds, a cold front may well be the cause: a sharp wind veer (in the northern hemisphere) will probably occur with squally conditions.

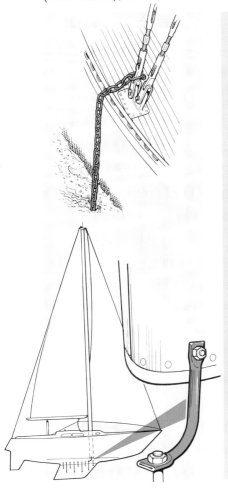

SOME POINTS TO CONSIDER ABOUT LIGHTNING

Lightning is always unpredictable. Though it will rarely strike a boat, enough cases exist, especially along the American eastern seaboard, to take all possible precautions. Since it will follow the most direct path to the water, it is up to you to provide such a path to help it on its way.

Though No. 8 copper wire is generally recommended for a lightning ground, another option is to use copper tubing, flattened at the ends connecting the lightning rod at the masthead with a keel bolt. In a boat with an encapsulated keel, a grounding plate should be attached to the hull as low below the waterline as is feasible.

The changing face of the sky gives a clear indication of any impending weather changes. Common sense dictates that you should learn to 'read' the sky and react in good time.

SAFETY AT SEA

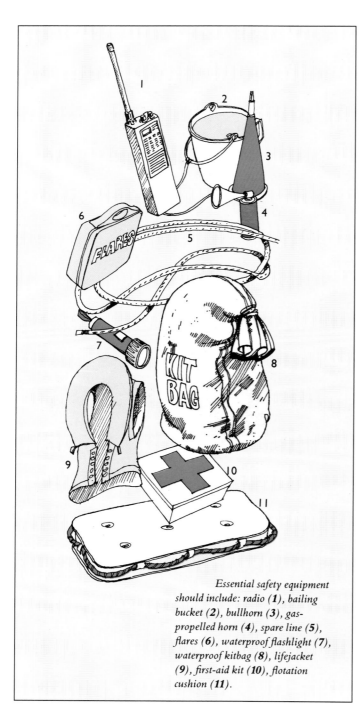

*Essential safety equipment should include: radio (**1**), bailing bucket (**2**), bullhorn (**3**), gas-propelled horn (**4**), spare line (**5**), flares (**6**), waterproof flashlight (**7**), waterproof kitbag (**8**), lifejacket (**9**), first-aid kit (**10**), flotation cushion (**11**).*

Few boats today are supplied fully equipped for sea, even if the builders sell them as 'sailaway'. Moreover, secondhand boats may be better equipped but they will still have gear which is in need of upgrading. The following things ought to be aboard:

BOW ROLLER These need to be stout, yet soft-mouthed and capable of taking sideways load as well as a fore-and-aft load. A pawl or ratchet can help to raise the anchor chain, by preventing what you have gained slipping back again.

WINDLASS If you anchor with chain, this will be a boon. There should be a reasonably long drop under the hawse pipe to prevent chain jams.

ANCHORS A main bow anchor and alternative style (possibly smaller) kedge are needed. Make sure they are securely stowed. If on the roller or deck chocks, use through-bolts or lashings. If in a bow well, the door should have a clasp.

DECK GEAR Large cleats make mooring much easier. If chain is used, they need to be higher off the deck. Cleats amidships will be needed for spring lines and where there is a cleat, a soft-mouthed fairlead is also necessary.

PULPIT A good pulpit will allow a crewman to sit on the lower rail and change sails with his back to the waves. The stern will need similar security from a taffrail or aft pulpit.

LIFELINES Double lifelines are better than single, and they should be carried on high stanchions secured in firm bases. Lifelines will need secured shackles or bottlescrews at the end in case of accidental collapse. and insulation to avoid 'close loop' radio interference.

LINES Four good length lines will be needed. As a guide, two of them should be one-and-a-half or two times the length of the boat.

STERN LADDER A transom ladder is useful for boarding high-sided boats from a dinghy or after a swim. They can also assist with a man overboard. To be of real benefit, the bottom rung should be well below the water's surface when lowered.

MAN-OVERBOARD EQUIPMENT The minimum should be a high-quality horseshoe buoy, preferably fitted with high-intensity light, whistle and dye marker. A second buoy, a 50-ft (15-m) floating heaving line and a dan-buoy can be added to the list.

HARNESS EYES Remaining on deck is vital. There should be safety harness attachment points by the companion-way and in the cockpit. Those on the centerline will help stop crew being washed overboard. Jackstays allow a person to move forward from bow to stern. The Latch-way Transfastener system is more refined, allowing greater freedom of movement.

NON-SLIP DECKS Secure footing is vital to safety, be it on stylish teak, non-slip paint or a proprietary finish such as Treadmaster. Moulded patterns in fiberglass decks are rarely good enough. Watch out for untreated areas on cockpit coamings, cabin tops etc. Hatches benefit from non-slip tape too.

HANDHOLDS These are vital for secure movement above and below decks. On deck they lead from cockpit to mast, at least; below, they should allow you to operate as normal with 20° of heel.

SAILS The standard mainsail should reef to at least 60% of its normal luff length. Storm sails should also be considered. If the jib is set in a luff foil some alternative means of attachment is a wise precaution.

NAVIGATION LIGHTS Showing the correct lights is a legal requirement at night and in poor visibility. Vessels up to 65ft (20m) can use either an electrically efficient mast-head tri-light or a bow mounted bi-light combined with a stern light. When motoring, a steaming light is mandatory if the boat is more than 22ft (7m) in length. This should be carried on the mast and show from full ahead to 22½° aft of the beam. Steaming lights should not be used in conjunction with tri-lights however.

NAVIGATION A VHF radio is both vital for listening to forecasts and a valuable means of summoning help in distress. Both the set and operator must be licensed. The antenna should be mounted as high as possible for maximum range. A spare emergency antenna is useful in case of dismasting. A cockpit speaker will allow the watch keeper to monitor the radio without disturbing those below. (See equipping the chart table page 59.)

SECURITY BELOWDECKS All heavy items should be secured below against the possibility of a 180° knockdown. This includes cookers. Batteries should be in leak-proof boxes sited out of the engine compartment.

GAS STOWAGE LPG gas is a convenient though potentially volatile fuel. Gas bottles should be stowed in overboard draining lockers. Cookers need flame-failure devices on each burner and all piping should be copper apart from short flexible spans. A shut-off cock at the galley is also needed.

FIRE FIGHTING Fire afloat is extremely dangerous and very frightening. All equipment must be sited so that fire in the galley or engine compartment (the most likely fire

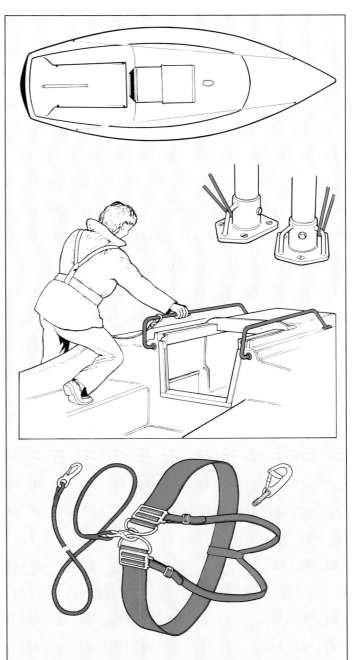

For a safety harness to be effective, jacklines as shown (TOP) are needed. They should be made up of plastic-coated wire securely attached. Hooking on to lifelines instead of jacklines can be guaranteed to throw you overboard, because they are so far outboard.

Another good idea is stainless-steel handrails on either side and around the companionway hatch (MIDDLE LEFT).

Stanchion bases (MIDDLE RIGHT) must be through-bolted and have high enough side walls to securely support the uprights. Also, there should be set screws to secure the stanchions, as well as bails to attach blocks, lines, fenders and such.

A reliable safety harness (ABOVE) will be very well constructed, with nonmagnetic metal parts, triple-stitched webbing and a nontripping safety hook.

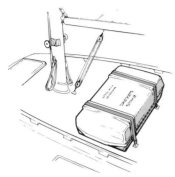

The liferaft should be mounted on deck. Too often it is shoved into a locker with assorted gear piled on top – not exactly where you want it when you need it. Forward or behind the mast is a good place in that it will allow a fairly clear platform to launch the raft. Remember always to attach the tether to a strongpoint on deck.

It's a good idea to keep a waterproof bag of emergency supplies just inside the companionway. This way, you'll have additional food and water, as well as any other navigational gear and survival equipment not included in the standard raft pack, should you abandon ship.

Ensign, horseshoe lifebuoys, and man-overboard lights.

the galley or engine compartment (the most likely fire sources) can be tackled quickly. A fire blanket can smother flame or protect the person. At least three 3lb (1.4kg) extinguishers should be carried. Dry powder types are non-toxic and can be used on all types of fire.

BILGE PUMPS These should be capable of use from the cockpit. Electric pumps should have a manual back-up. A portable pump will help reach awkward parts, while pick-up pipes need a strainer or strum box to prevent clogging.

FLARES These must be 'in-date' and carried in a waterproof container. Four white and four red hand flares are the minimum for inshore sailing. Offshore, four red parachute flares and two orange smoke flares should be carried as well.

FIRST AID KIT AND MANUAL All items used must be replaced. You will need to deal with seasickness, headaches, upset stomachs, sunburn, constipation and perhaps breakages and flesh wounds.

TOOL KIT Pliers, adjustable wrench, spanners, Allen keys, Philips and cross-head screwdrivers, hacksaw, drill and bits will form a good basis. Carry plenty of spares for electrical equipment, the engine, winches and the boat (blocks, bottlescrews, shackles, self-tapping screws, nuts, bolts, washers etc.). Every kit should have PVC or duct tape, WD40 spray or equivalent, sealant and underwater epoxy.

SAIL REPAIR KIT Sewing palm, needles, whipping twine, spinnaker repair tape and self-adhesive sail cloth are needed here.

PERSONAL SAFETY

The skipper should ensure that safety gear is provided for his crew but there is no substitute for having your own correctly fitting equipment which you know how to operate.

For personal buoyancy, choose either a lifejacket or a buoyancy aid. The difference is explained by their respective names. A buoyancy aid is just a means to keep you afloat though often they are more practical, stylish and still enjoy approval by regulatory bodies.

A lifejacket on the other hand has a sufficient amount of buoyancy correctly distributed behind the head and on the chest to float the wearer face up away from the direction of the oncoming waves even if he or she is unconscious. Lifejackets are bulky so some sailors use gas or oral inflation types which lie flat against the body although they do require a conscious operator if they are to be of any use. Some inflate automatically on contact with water.

Wearing a safety harness should preempt such problems as it aims to keep the wearer attached to the boat should he stumble or be swept overboard. The harness should be adjusted to fit over oilskins and be easy to don – even in the dark. Choose a make which offers a positive latch on the snapshackle at the end of the lifeline. Gibb makes a snapshackle used worldwide, and a catch on it has to be released before the shackle will open, whereas normal snapshackles can open themselves if attached to an eyebolt.

Wearing a harness should be routine at night or in rough conditions. But a cumbersome harness and lifejacket together can interfere in the operation of each other. This is why the top-of-the-line gear either have built-in flotation as a substitute for a lifejacket or they offer a specially matched lifejacket which attaches to the outside of the jacket. Combine this with a built-in harness and there is no reason not to use personal safety gear as soon as it is needed. Too often, during a sail change for instance, sailors find excuses not to don a harness.

FIRE HAZARDS

The auxiliary engine in a large keelboat is a potential hazard, especially if it uses gasoline as a fuel. Gas fumes tend to gather in a boat's bilge, and a skipper must make sure the boat is thoroughly ventilated before starting the engine or working near the bilge.

Fire extinguishers should be placed in key locations throughout the boat. If your boat has a galley stove, make sure there's a fire extinguisher near by but *not* above the stove; in a flare-up, the extinguisher must be accessible, not engulfed in flame. It is wise to mount an automatic extinguishing system (CO_2 or Halon 1301) within the engine compartment for on-the-spot protection, but also important to have hand-operated extinguishers nearby.

A gas-engined boat should have forced-air circulation for the bilge – a blower to pull fumes out of the lowest point in the bilge area, but it's a good idea to have the same system in a diesel boat if only to keep the area cool.

DISTRESS

The most important piece of safety gear aboard may be your bilge pump. Do not trust merely one to do the job. Your boat should have an electrical bilge pump, driven off the ship's battery system, an additional manual pump and even a third pump, this one driven off the engine and capable of pumping the greatest volume possible with the power available.

There may come a time when long-distance communication is required to get help in a crisis. Learn how to use the VHF radio, and know the common distress frequencies.

Always check your transmitting capabilities at the beginning of a sail. Ask for a radio check on the common-traffic channel, and always ask the respondent for his approximate position, so that you know how far you've managed to transmit. In any routine communications, take note of your communications range and the quality of your reception and transmission.

Have a suitable signal-flare system aboard. No less than ten skyrocket flares, plus another ten hand-held flares are considered adequate. Day signals consist of smoke flares and/or bright shapes or flags.

If you spend long periods of time far offshore, a reputable inflatable liferaft is a good idea. If you do venture offshore, but not that frequently, then your normal ship's tender (your dinghy) could serve in an emergency. Whichever you choose, you should have a kit made up for the chance that you'll have to take to your raft or dinghy. The kit should include, at very least, *(1)* A strong waterproof light. *(2)* A complete first-aid kit. *(3)* A complete flare kit. *(4)* Throwable lifesaving device. *(5)* Some lengths of synthetic line. *(6)* Minimal rations. *(7)* A portable EPIRB – or emergency position-indicating radio beacon.

A hand-held radio-telephone can be a life saver but is generally unnecessary in areas of high traffic. A bright-colored flag or shape for hand-signalling would certainly be less expensive, and might serve the purpose as well. At night, a stick flare could be used to attract attention in an emergency.

Remember that too much gear can be a hindrance aboard a small boat. Make sure you have the space to stow securely the equipment you bring along, and make sure you bring those things you'll really need before you start loading up with extras.

CLOTHING

Cold, wet: *tired*. The converse is true. Warm, dry: *alert*. How do you best stay that way? Most experts agree on two dressing procedures: first, wear layers of relatively light clothing; second, wear natural fibers, particularly cotton and wool. The importance of good clothing should not be underestimated. Heat loss is quite marked even in low wind speeds so a wind-proof outer layer is essential. A waterproof layer is vital too, for wet clothing has only 10% of the insulation value of dry clothing.

The most important insulator is free and available in limitless quantities. It is air, and how it is trapped accounts for much of the thermal property of most materials.

The choice these days is between man-made fibers and natural materials. It is an argument not fully resolved and most sailors find themselves wearing some combination of the two. Eiderdown may offer the greatest heat insulation, up to 90% of its theoretical maximum, but it is very expensive and of little use when it is wet. Wool has long been a favorite, particularly in its oiled form, but it is slow drying and smelly when wet.

Natural materials are still a good foundation until conditions warrant oilskins. Denim jeans are best avoided because once damp they take a very long time to dry. Their close-fitting styling makes kneeling and bending difficult. Loose-fitting trousers, a good thick cotton or wool shirt and pullover are best.

For the layer next to the skin, thermal underwear is available. Instead of using cotton, which absorbs body moisture, most manufacturers use something artificial such as polypropylene or polyester fleece which transfers moisture away – a process known as 'wicking'. When working on deck in oilskins it is very easy to work up a sweat and a moisture-transfer process is a comfortable alternative to cotton. Both T-shirts and long-john trousers are available in these materials.

The layer between this foundation and the outer oilskins is often a fiber-pile garment available worldwide – Helly Hansen, Land's End, L. L. Bean, Patagonia and Chuck Roast are just some of their makers. The pile in these garments traps air making them great insulators and now that they often have a finely-woven outer shell, they afford good wind resistance when conditions do not warrant an oilskin jacket.

In warm air and a dry breeze they can dry out in a few hours and even putting them on wet is not unbearable. For overnight sailing, lined PVC trousers can keep the bottom half nice and snug.

If another layer is needed on top, consider a vest. These are now very stylish for après sail and they retain body warmth underneath oilskins without further limiting arm movement.

Foul weather gear will most likely be the most expensive purchase and the more you pay the better the garments will be. Trousers should be chest-high to keep the wind away from the gap between waist-high trousers and the jacket. They should also have a means of securing the ankles to keep out water. A pocket and an opening fly are always useful provided that they do not compromise the trousers' watertight integrity.

Jackets are more convenient if they are zipped at the front rather than being an over-the-head style anorak (windbreaker). There should be flaps both on the inside and outside to seal off the zip. Like the trousers, the wrist opening should be capable of being sealed against the arm. Plenty of pockets are useful for handkerchiefs, knives, torches and so on.

Top of the range foulweather gear for offshore sailing, with reflective patches and built-in harness.

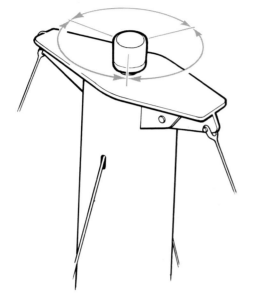

Regulation masthead tri-color lights (ABOVE) are far more visible than traditional pulpit-mounted ones, which are liable not to be seen through the waves. Remember to replace the bulb at the start of each season. The last thing you want to do is clamber up the mast on a rainy night.

The safety harness (RIGHT) should be worn on deck in difficult conditions.
Safety harness tether lines (BELOW RIGHT). Note that the bottom hook has a double action to prevent accidental opening.

As you spend more the garments should offer more refinements: a built-in close-fitting hood with fasteners rather than ties which are awkward to use with cold hands; a lining to cut down condensation, perhaps even a closed-cell buoyancy lining; hand warmer pockets; a built-in safety harness; crotch strap; reflective patches for man-overboard situations. Top-of-the-range garments will also have reinforced knees, seats and elbows. The manufacturers will have taken special care to cut the garment to avoid seams in highly stressed areas such as the shoulders and seat to ensure they remain consistently and fully watertight.

This clothing is made in two main types of material: polyurethane-proofed woven nylon and PVC. Woven nylon generally stows more compactly and is more supple and lighter to wear. It needs frequent washing to remove ingrained salt. Some makers offer a winter re-proofing service. PVC is thought to be tougher and more abrasion resistant. Small tears can be taped or welded with glue. Most PVC suits are heavy to wear and carry.

HEAD, HANDS AND FEET

It is often the extremities which suffer the cold first and for longest. The head can lose as much heat as the body can produce, so something worn up top can make the whole body feel warmer. A skiing-style hat is ideal, while a balaclava is excellent for more extreme conditions.

Hands must be kept warm and protected. Until they are hardened with regular sailing, leather gloves will protect soft palms. Those with open backs do not offer much warmth and, unless there is double thickness on the inside of the palms and fingers, such gloves will have a very short life handling halyards, sheets and anchor cable or chain.

Fingerless gloves will still allow you to tie knots and undo shackles. For longer periods of inactivity a pair of mittens can make even the chilliest of watches a little more comfortable.

As for the feet, there is no substitute for a good pair of boots. They should be high so that you can work on deck or step ashore from a dinghy without filling them up. The soles should afford a good grip and be non-marking. This generally means that flat soles are best so that ankles are not turned as you tread on the irregularities of the deck and its gear.

Many people believe in having boots a size larger than normal footwear. The air space creates insulation and permits the wearing of a thicker or second pair of socks.

As for shoes, most leisure shoes will suffice. The more support they offer, the better. Other points to look for are a good grip and a sole which neither picks up too much debris which is then walked onboard nor marks. Certain running shoes have black soles and are not suitable.

Leather moccasin styles (Docksiders, Topsiders are two of the better-known brands) are very popular among sailors and have the advantage that the leather, stitching and other parts are all salt-water resistant.

STAYING AWAKE

The 1972 COLREGS (International Regulations for Avoiding Collision at Sea) are quite explicit: all ships must post a lookout at all times. That many don't and that the seas of the world are filled with wrecks should be warning enough to any sailor. If you are sailing alone, you can duck below for a few moments to get food, plot position and such, but your visible horizon must be clear of traffic even for that.

How do you prevent fatigue? And what can you do about it once it's come on? The answer to both questions is simple . . . sleep.

A safe rule to follow is that when you're nearer to shore than 50 miles (80km), stay awake, and stay in the

(LEFT): Although it is tempting when over-tired, excessive amounts of coffee does not keep you awake. You will only feel tense and nervous, which, combined with fatigue, could impair your ability to make safe judgements.

cockpit or wheelhouse. Further out – except in port approaches such as Boston Harbor, San Francisco Bay, anything along the southern coast of England, off Durban, and so on – a certain amount of sleep is a safer bet, but you can never be sure when a ship will come over the horizon and 'discover' you.

Modern boats do not heave-to well, so you will either have to stay awake or else anchor for the night. The risks are too great to suggest anything else.

As the body wakes up, it burns energy at an astonishing rate, especially when engaged in strenuous tasks. If possible, have everything aboard and set to take off the day before you plan to leave. Rest your muscles as well as your brain. Have a hearty, but not rich, meal at least three hours before you board your boat. Keep fruit and crackers handy to the helm for your first nourishment on board. Most important, eat when hungry, not when you feel you *should*. Keeping a constant level of food-supplied energy and blood sugar is important for continuing physical and mental effectiveness.

Don't drink alcohol. Don't drink carbonated beverages. Don't eat greasy or heavily sugared foods. Not initially, at any rate. Try to eat a lot of roughage – greens, lettuce, bran and such. The change of environment and habit is likely to cause constipation, which will not only cause discomfort but also add to the fatigue problem.

Excessive amounts of coffee will *not* keep you alert. It may keep you up, but the tension it produces, added to your existing anxiety over the impending voyage, will probably cause ill-considered judgments.

Likewise, no drugs of any kind (unless necessary for health) should be taken before or during sailing.

Under way, the greatest threat to staying awake is staying on the helm. Sure, it's fun and exciting to steer your ship through wind and waves. It is also tiring, something like driving a car for 10 hours. If you have fitted auto-steering or can rig a sheet-to-tiller rig, use it whenever you're not in congested waters.

CHAPTER TEN

RULES OF THE ROAD

SOUND SIGNALS

SOUND SIGNALS

POWER DRIVEN VESSELS IN SIGHT OF EACH OTHER	
●	I am altering course to starboard
● ●	I am altering course to port
● ● ●	I am going astern
● ● ● ● ●	I fail to understand your intention or action; or I do not think that you are taking sufficient action to avoid collision
●	Warning by vessel approaching a bend
VESSELS IN REDUCED VISIBILITY	
●	Power driven vessel making way
● ●	Power driven vessel stopped or not making way
● ● ●	Sailing vessel or powered vessel restricted in its ability to manoeuvre, constrained by draught, under tow, or engaged in fishing

KEY ● denotes approximately 1 second ● denotes 4–6 seconds

BASIC RULES OF THE ROAD

Wind

1 A boat on port tack gives way to one on starboard tack

2 An overtaking boat must give way to the overtaken boat

3 If two boats are running downwind, the one on starboard tack has right of way

4 A boat running downwind gives way to one close-hauled

Considering that man has been at sea since prehistory, it is surprising that the rules of the road were only formalized just over 100 years ago.

The International Regulations for the Prevention of Collision at Sea is the seaman's Highway Code. It is a complex, binding document which deals with every situation a vessel is likely to encounter, both on the high sea and arms of the sea.

The rules themselves are a masterpiece of drafting with each word having a precise meaning. 'May' gives the seaman an option while 'shall' and 'must' are mandatory. While the rules may appear daunting – there are 38 of them, each with many subsections – they do correspond to general common sense and seamanship.

Learning the rules word-perfect would be almost impossible, but every sailor is urged to study them in depth in order to appreciate fully their spirit and to learn the significance of lights, shapes and sound signals and the responses they require from those at sea.

Many national sailing authorities publish the full Collision Regulations with special annotation explaining points of special relevance.

There are basically two types of rule:

1. Those which tell the sailor what to carry and how and when to use it. Some of these rules tell other mariners who you are, where you are, what you are doing and where you are going;

2. Those which tell the other mariner what his course of action should be, so that he can tell you what he is, where he is, what he is doing and where he is going.

This distinction between the two parties is fundamental to the Collision Regulations.

The rules are in four sections: General; Steering and Sailing Rules; Lights and Shapes; Sound and Light Signals. What follows is an abridged version of the main rules. The rules themselves are in italics.

PART A – GENERAL
RULE 1 – APPLICATION

These rules shall apply to all vessels on the high seas and waters connected therewith, navigable by sea-going vessels.

Common sense dictates that a sail boat should keep clear of all commercial vessels, especially large ships with limited maneuverability.

RULE 2 – RESPONSIBILITY

Nothing shall exonerate any vessel or the owner, master and crew from the consequences of neglect. In complying with these rules due regard shall be given to all dangers of navigation and collision and to any special circumstances which may make a departure from these rules necessary to avoid immediate danger.

PART B – STEERING AND SAILING RULES

SECTION 1 – APPLIED IN ANY CONDITION OF VISIBILITY

RULE 5 – LOOKOUT

Every vessel shall maintain at all times, a proper lookout by sight and hearing as well as by all available means appropriate to the circumstances.

This is probably the single most important rule. On boats you must be aware of the blind spots such as behind the leeward side of the headsail or behind the structure if keeping watch for long periods from an inside steering position. It is also important to preserve night vision from bright interior lights, cigarette lighters and deck floodlights because 100 per cent night vision is lost in a fraction of a second, yet takes many minutes to recover. Note also the reference to hearing. In fog, for example, a lookout away from engine and exhaust noise is invaluable.

RULE 6 – SAFE SPEED

Every vessel shall proceed at a safe speed so that she can take proper and effective action to avoid collision.

Many factors should be taken into account here: level of visibility, traffic density, maneuverability of vessels, depth of water, presence of background lights at night and state of wind, sea and tide.

RULE 7 – RISK OF COLLISION

In determining if the risk of collision exists, the following shall be among the considerations taken into account: if the compass bearing of an approaching vessel does not alter appreciably or if approaching is a very large vessel, a tow or vessel at close range.

Here there can be no substitute for taking a bearing on an approaching vessel and monitoring any change closely thereafter.

RULE 8 – ACTION TO AVOID COLLISION

Action to avoid collision shall be positive, made in ample time and with due regard to good seamanship.

This often means making your intentions clear early. In giving way to one vessel do not increase the risk of collision with another. In confined waters such alterations of course may often take small craft out of the buoyed deep-water channels.

RULE 9 – NARROW CHANNELS

A vessel proceeding along the course of a narrow channel or fairway shall keep as near to the outer limit of the channel as is safe and practicable. A vessel less than 20 meters or engaged in fishing, shall not impede the passage of any other vessel and any vessel shall if possible avoid anchoring in the channel.

The definition of a narrow channel is purposely avoided. In what may seem a large body of water to the sailor, the professional mariner has to maneuver his merchant vessel with the utmost precision, while the area needed by a passenger liner to adjust speed or course is enormous.

RULE 10—TRAFFIC SEPARATION SCHEMES

A vessel so far as practicable shall avoid crossing traffic lanes, but if obliged to do so, shall cross as nearly as practicable at right-angles to the general direction of traffic flow. A vessel less than 20 meters or a sailing vessel shall not impede the safe passage of a power-driven vessel following a traffic lane.

This last part may seem in conflict with the idea that power gives way to sail, but it should be obvious that a smaller vessel ought to keep clear of a larger one in an area of high traffic density. Also take special note of the instruction to cross at right-angles. This means the boat's heading (ie course steered) should be at right-angles to the traffic lane, not her course over the ground.

There are two reasons for this. Firstly, simple geometry tells us that even if a boat crabs sideways on a tide, she will cross through the lane quicker if she steers straight across rather than steering into the tide.

Secondly her aspect, particularly her lights at night, will show others that her intention is to cross at right-angles. Traffic separation lanes are becoming increasingly frequent so our behavior in them warrants extra thought.

SECTION 2 – CONDUCT OF VESSELS IN SIGHT OF ONE ANOTHER

RULE 12—SAILING VESSELS

When two vessels are approaching one another, so as to involve the risk of collision, one of them shall keep out of the way of the other as follows:
i) When each has the wind on a different side, the vessel which has the wind on her port side shall keep clear.
ii) When both have the wind on the same side, the vessel which is to windward shall keep out of the way of the vessel to leeward.
iii) If a vessel with the wind on the port sees a vessel to windward and cannot determine with certainty whether' the other has the wind on the starboard side, she shall keep out of the way of the other.

RULE 13—OVERTAKING

Notwithstanding anything contained in the rules of this section, any overtaking vessel shall keep out of the way of the vessel being overtaken. A vessel shall be deemed to be overtaking when coming on another vessel from a direction more than 22.5 degrees abaft her beam. If a vessel should be in doubt as to whether she is overtaking or not, she should assume this is the case. Any subsequent alteration of the bearing between the two vessels shall not make the overtaking vessel a crossing vessel within the meaning of the rules.

This rule cautions the helmsman to assess the effect of a course alteration before it is made.

RULE 14—HEAD-ON SITUATION

When two power-driven vessels are meeting on a reciprocal course or nearly reciprocal courses, each shall alter her course to starboard so that each shall pass on the port side of the other.

For the purposes of the rules, a boat using her auxiliary engine is considered a power-driven vessel.

RULE 15—CROSSING SITUATION

When two power-driven vessels are crossing as to involve the risk of collision, the vessel which has the other on her starboard side shall keep out of the way and shall, if the circumstances of the case permit, avoid crossing ahead of the other vessel.

One circumstance where this might apply is if a third ship or navigation hazard prevents an alteration to starboard.

RULE 16—ACTION BY GIVE-WAY VESSEL

Every vessel which is directed to keep clear of another vessel shall, so far as possible, take early and substantial action to keep well clear.

RULE 17—ACTION BY STAND-ON VESSEL

a) Where one of two vessels is to keep out of the way, the other shall keep her course and speed. The latter vessel however may take action to avoid collision by her manoeuvre alone, as soon as it becomes apparent to her that the vessel required to keep out of the way is not taking the appropriate action.

This rule may seem contradictory in that it requires the right-of-way vessel to maintain her course and speed but allows her to take avoiding action and ultimately requires her to avoid collision. The key is that it allows the stand-on vessel with rights, to take avoiding action if the give-way vessel fails to act in accordance with the rules. Thus a boat should not hold on into danger just because the rules say she has right of way.

RULE 18—RESPONSIBILITIES BETWEEN VESSELS

Except where rules 9, 10 and 13 otherwise require:
a) a power-driven vessel under way shall keep out of the way of a vessel not under command: a vessel restricted in her ability to move; a vessel engaged in fishing; a sailing vessel.
b) a sailing vessel shall keep clear of a vessel not under command; one restricted in her ability to maneuver; or one engaged in fishing.
c) a fishing vessel shall keep clear of vessels not under command and vessels with restricted ability maneuver.

NAVIGATION LIGHTS
AND SHAPES

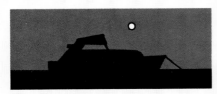

1 At anchor. All-round white light.

2 At anchor. Black ball forward.

3 Motor sailing. Cone, point down, forward.

4 Divers down. Letter 'A' International Code.

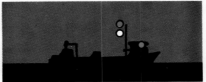

5 Vessel fishing. All-round red light over all-round white.

6 Fishing/trawling. Two cones point to point, or a basket if less than 20m.

7 Vessels being towed and towing. Towed vessel shows side-lights (forward) and sternlight. Vessel towing shows two masthead lights, sidelights, sternlight, yellow towing light.

8 Towing by day. Length of tow more than 200m. Both vessels display diamond shapes. By night the towing vessel shows three masthead lights instead of two.

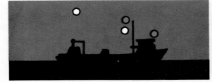

9 Vessel trawling. All-round green light over all-round white.

10 Pilot boat. All-round white light over all-round red.

11 Restricted maneuverability. All-round red, white, red lights vertically.

12 Restricted maneuverability. Ball, diamond, ball vertically.

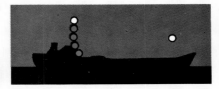

13 Constrained by draft. Three all-round red lights. By day, a cylinder.

CHAPTER ELEVEN

FLAGS AND THEIR USES

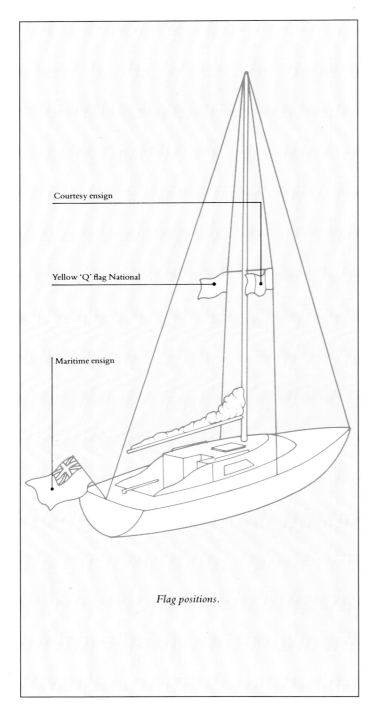

Courtesy ensign

Yellow 'Q' flag National

Maritime ensign

Flag positions.

Courtesy on the water is something which sailors value highly. As the pace of life becomes more frenetic ashore, the goodwill experienced in the company of other sailors is valued more highly than ever.

More custom surrounds flags than probably any other facet of yachting, and few subjects occupy yarning sailors more than precisely the 'right' way to do things.

One fact, however, is certain: of all flags flown it is the ensign which denotes the nationality of the boat and her owner and the use of the national maritime flag is governed by law around the world. Today though, establishing the actual nationality of the owner is not so straightforward, for many yachts are company owned. It is common for large luxury motor yachts to fly an American flag, for example, because of the status it brings, though the company owning the yacht may be foreign-owned.

For small pleasure craft, flying their country's maritime ensign is usually optional unless they are documented. At sea, the ensign (or colors) is flown during daylight hours. In port, the hours are considered to be 0800 until 2100 or sunset, whichever is soonest. It is the traditional practice to take one's time for making colors and for striking them from naval vessels which might be in port or from the senior yacht club. Sadly, many of today's owners leave their ensign flying all day, all night and even when they pack up and leave the boat.

Some boats have the right to wear special status ensigns. In Britain, for example, a special Admiralty warrant can be obtained to wear the White Ensign or the Blue or Red Ensign which have been 'defaced' with a club crest. Such privilege ensigns can only be flown when the owner is on board.

Ensigns are the most important flags a boat can fly, so they should be flown in the most prominent position. Surprisingly this is the aft end, not the bow, dating from the time when sailing ships were commanded from the quarter deck. On a sloop, a staff on the taffrail can be used. Yawls and ketches use a staff on top of the mizzen mast, while gaff-rigged sloops and schooners attach the ensign two-thirds up the leech of the aftermost sail.

When visiting foreign waters it is courteous to fly the maritime ensign of that country. It should be smaller than the boat's own national flag and flown in an inferior position. Most often, this will mean from the starboard spreader. When entering foreign waters for the first time or when returning to home waters from abroad, the yellow Flag 'Q' should be flown from the port spreaders This indicates a request for Customs clearance.

It is a custom to salute royal yachts and warships of all countries and yachts belonging to the flag officers of the owner's own club. Fortunately the latter has only to be done once in a day. To make a salute, the ensign is 'dipped'. This entails lowering the ensign to a little lower than half hoist and keeping it there until the vessel being saluted responds in similar fashion. When the latter re-hoists her ensign, the saluting vessel follows suit.

The notion of seniority governs the use of other flags. Yachts often fly their club burgees (small triangular flags) at the masthead and if an owner belongs to more than one, he should fly the burgee of the more senior club, or the club whose home port he is visiting. Most yacht clubs have special flags for their officers, based on the club burgee. The commodore can fly a broad or swallow-tailed pennant (long tapered flag) while those belonging to the vice- and rear-commodores are distinguished by one or two balls being added to the design.

DRESSING SHIP

If a full set of International Code flags are carried a yacht may 'dress ship'. This is decorative and can be done on special holidays. Other occasions are festivals at home and abroad and local events, such as club regattas or cruising meets. There are few finer sights than a yacht dressed from stem to masthead to stern.

Dressing ship for the club regatta.

The preferred order from bow to stern uses signal flags and numeral pennants. The suggested order is:
E Q p3 G p8 z p4 W p6 P p1 I Code T Y B X 1st H 3rd D F 2nd U A O M R p2 J p0 N p9 K p7 V p5 L C S

This cutter-rigged ketch is so low and sleek that perhaps its outsize 'red duster' is not inappropriate.

CHAPTER TWELVE

EMERGENCY!

There are several ways of signalling for help and these should be used only when the situation demands. Even with the high number of 'false alarms', most rescue services would prefer warning to be given early enough for them to respond in time.

CALLING FOR HELP:
DISTRESS SIGNALLING

VHF radio is perhaps the most commonly used means for indicating distress. Before you transmit you will need to know your position, which may be given as either latitude and longitude or, more simply, a distance bearing from a known landmark or object. Transmit on Channel 16 at full power, following this procedure:

- the distress signal MAYDAY MAYDAY MAYDAY
- the name or other identification of the vessel in distress
- particulars of her position
- the nature of distress and the kind of assistance required
- any other information which may facilitate the rescue
- the invitation to reply and acknowledge

If no reply is received, check the equipment and repeat at regular intervals on the same or any channel.

Hand-held pyrotechnics must be used with care, away from sails and with foreknowledge. Many manufacturers now make practice flares, which are legal for testing your skills.

If the safety of the boat or person is not in immediate danger a less urgent message may be broadcast using the signal PAN PAN instead of MAYDAY.

If out of VHF range, or in mid-ocean, use either MF radio on the distress frequency of 2182kHz or activate the EPIRB (Emergency Position-Indicating Radio Beacon) which operates on aircraft frequencies.

If no radio is required visual signals can be used. These include: raising and lowering your arms slowly; thick, black smoke generated by burning oily rags; an ensign hoisted upside down; a square flag with a ball, or similar, above or below it; or the morse code SOS (...---...).

The following International Code flags have specific meanings:

F I am disabled	W I require medical
V I require assistance	assistance
O Man overboard	NC I am in distress and
	require assistance

Lastly, virtually all boats carry flares. They both draw attention to the boat and help locate it. White flares are for collision warnings, red flares are distress signals. There are three types of flares, namely: parachute rockets which reach 1000ft (300m) and which burn for 40 seconds; red hand flares which burn for 40 seconds; and buoyant orange smoke signals which burn for three minutes.

They should be used in the following order: two red parachute rockets fired two minutes apart, the first to attract attention and the second for verification. You should then wait at least 40 minutes for a response before firing more. If a vessel or helicopter is sighted, identify yourself with the red hand flare. The buoyant orange signal is also used for identification from the air.

At night a search aircraft may fire a green flare to which a red hand flare can be used as a response.

There are three musts in using flares. They *must* be in date. You *must* read the instructions. You *must* fire them downwind. Hand flares generate a lot of smoke and heat while parachute rockets are specially designed to assume an upwind trajectory. When there is low cloud cover, angle the rockets down to no more than 45°.

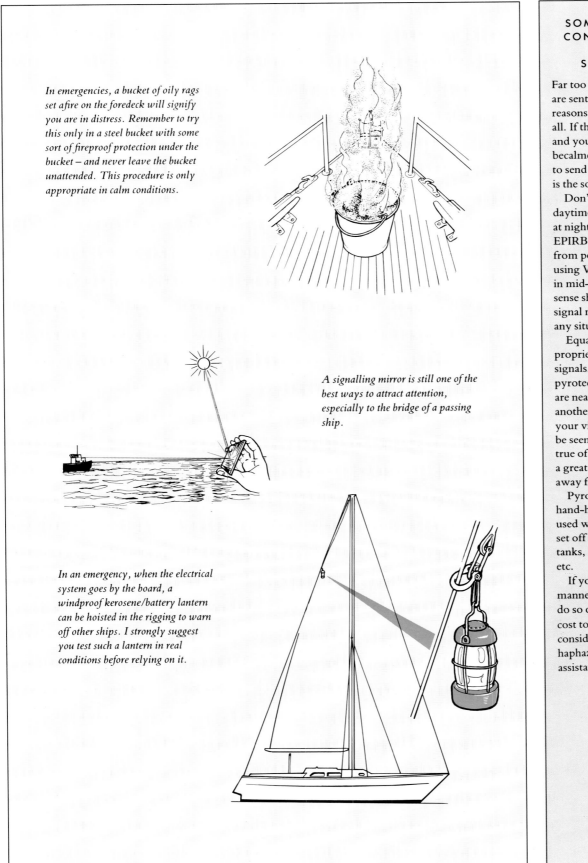

In emergencies, a bucket of oily rags set afire on the foredeck will signify you are in distress. Remember to try this only in a steel bucket with some sort of fireproof protection under the bucket – and never leave the bucket unattended. This procedure is only appropriate in calm conditions.

A signalling mirror is still one of the best ways to attract attention, especially to the bridge of a passing ship.

In an emergency, when the electrical system goes by the board, a windproof kerosene/battery lantern can be hoisted in the rigging to warn off other ships. I strongly suggest you test such a lantern in real conditions before relying on it.

SOME POINTS TO CONSIDER ABOUT DISTRESS SIGNALLING

Far too often distress signals are sent for inappropriate reasons or for no reason at all. If the engine has died and you are merely becalmed, *no* reason exists to send any signal. Patience is the solution.

Don't use flares in the daytime and smoke signals at night. Don't use an EPIRB when 5 miles (8km) from port. Don't attempt using VFH distress channel in mid-ocean. Common sense should dictate the signal most appropriate for any situation.

Equally a question of propriety, don't waste signals, especially pyrotechnics. Unless you are near land, or sight another ship, chances are your visual signal will not be seen. This is especially true of open water passages, a great many of which are away from shipping lanes.

Pyrotechnics, either hand-held or fired, must be used with caution. Always set off flares away from tanks, gas bottles, engines, etc.

If you can – whatever the manner – get safely to port, do so on your own. The cost to others must be considered before haphazardly requesting assistance.

MAN OVERBOARD

Losing a person over the side is probably the situation sailors fear most. Most crews will have had some experience of recovering a hat or bucket dropped overboard and will have realized the difficulties even in fair conditions. Practicing man overboard drill is, therefore, an important safety precaution and the skipper is well advised to get other members of the crew to learn how to handle the boat under such circumstances, in case it is the skipper himself who is lost over the side. A good idea is to design a simple sling system – perhaps using the boom vang, topping lift, mainsheet, or some separate tackle – for strapping around the man in the water and swinging him aboard (see below right). There are many other methods.

A cry of 'Man overboard' will alert the whole crew. Anyone below deck should press the appropriate button on the sophisticated navigation aid such as Loran, which will pinpoint the position and allow the vessel to return to the same spot. Failing this, a careful note of compass heading and log reading or time should achieve the same result. Simultaneously, on deck, the lifebelt should be thrown and, if fitted, the dan-buoy as well. A crew member should be detailed to watch the person all the time as the head and shoulders of a person in the water can be quickly lost from sight from even a slow moving boat sailing in fair conditions.

Return to the person in the water as quickly as possible. If a spinnaker is set or the jib is poled out, these must be cleared away immediately. With the boat under normal sail again, she can be tacked or gybed on to a reciprocal course. Some skippers prefer to gybe as this takes the boat downwind so that the person can then be approached on a close reach. Tacking may be safer if conditions are difficult and is less likely to disorientate the inexperienced crew. Either way, the object is to approach the person from windward, ideally bringing the boat to a halt with the wind spilt from the sails, and with the person on the lower side – the boat's leeward beam. This calls for precise control of speed and course.

There is no reason why the engine could not be used but make absolutely certain that there are no sheets or ropes over the side to foul the propeller. To do so could inhibit the boat from sailing back to the lost crew member.

Recovering the person from the water can be even more difficult. If the victim is still conscious and mobile, he might be able to climb up the stern ladder or use a rope looped over the side. If he is helpless, the difficulties are immense. It may be possible for another member of the crew to slip into the water (provided they are tethered to the boat and wearing a lifejacket),

In dealing with a man overboard, throwing the horseshoe lifebuoy to the crew member in distress is a first priority (TOP).

The one good method for recovering a man overboard is to attach the luff of a sail to the gunwale. A halyard is fixed to the clew and the sail lowered in the water like a scoop. Even a weak victim may be able to hold himself in the sail as it is raised on the halyard

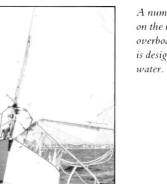

A number of clever devices are now on the market for recovering a man overboard. This rigid loop (LEFT) is designed to lasso the man in the water.

(BOTTOM). *As the sail is raised it draws the person closer to the boat and also increases in area to form a bigger envelope.*

It may also be possible to use the boom and mainsheet as a crane, but only if the topping lift is strong enough. Practice different methods in calm waters until you find one that works and become familiar with it.

to slip a safety harness or bowline around the victim. He can also be winched aboard using the main halyard. Such assistance should not be attempted if there is a chance of adding an additional problem to the first emergency.

SOLO SAILOR OVERBOARD

For a singlehander, nothing is more terrifying than going overboard. No man-overboard drills practiced with crew mean a damn thing. Prior preparation and practice is vital to saving one's life.

Assuming you've done everything possible to stay in the boat, what happens if you still flip over the side? You've got to get back on board. Unless you're hand steering, the boat will continue on its merry way, not having any response to weather helm.

Precautions to take for getting back aboard include:

First, trail a polypropylene line – 50 to 100 feet (15 to 30 metres) long – from a stern cleat. Tie a small buoy to the trailing end. Poly lines float, and if you can find one in a Day-Glo color, all the better.

Second, mount a ladder that is reachable from the stern. It can be a drop-down stainless steel one, or a rope with a release line. Assuming the boat is whizzing along at 5 or 6 knots, you will, with all your clothes, have a very difficult time hauling yourself to the stern. You will be exhausted. Even climbing a ladder will be a Herculean feat.

Provided you are able to get back on board, you will be exhausted, cold, very wet and possibly on the verge of shock. If you're in clear waters, get below instantly, get out of *all* your clothes, put on the heaviest, warmest things you've got, especially for your feet and hands, and get something warm into your stomach. Don't drink alcohol! But soup, tea or cocoa will warm you with no after effects. Drink slowly and give your body time to build up its temperature again.

RUNNING AGROUND

Going aground is an everyday hazard, but not always serious unless it is caused by inaccurate navigation or carelessness. It can range from a soft grounding on a sandbar, to a hard and potentially damaging crunch on a reef or rocky coast.

The best cure is prevention: keep track of your position on the up-to-date charts; know the depth under your keel, either by sounding with a leadline or an electronic depth sounder; and take the time to acquire local knowledge from fishermen.

If you should go aground, the immediate reaction of the helmsman should be to spin the boat around and see if she will come off the way she went on. If this fails, drop the sails to prevent her from driving on further, if it is a lee shore. On a weather shore, hoisting more sail may do the trick.

If the tide is flooding you may be floated free very quickly. If it is falling you may be in for a long wait until the next high tide. The worst possible situation is to go aground at high water during a spring tide: then you may have to wait until the cycle of tides runs through neaps and back into springs, some two weeks later. If the tide is falling, it is a good idea to heel the boat toward the shore. This should not only make her sit more upright but lean the cockpit away from the incoming sea. It can be done by sending one or two agile crewmen out on the boom as it is swung far to one side. Another anchor may also be set out to the side and the main halyard attached to its line. Then the halyard is hauled and the boat further heeled until the kedge can spin her off the bottom (see below). There might be time to use cushions and sailbags to pad nasty looking rocks as the boat heels toward them.

Several techniques may be used to get the boat off. One is to take an anchor out in the dinghy and then lead the rode to a winch via a block; another is to reduce the draft by suspending heavy weights such as jerry cans on the boom. Sinking the bow may also reduce draft, depending on the shape of the boat. If a boat has twin keels, however, remember it will draw less water upright than when heeled.

Your gear should include a *kedge,* or heavy anchor with stout line long enough to set for hauling off the bar or reef. If your boat has a standard Danforth or plow, either can be used as a kedge, provided it is heavy enough.

The kedge is taken out in the ship's tender to a point in deeper water, and set. Strain is taken, and the boat is pivoted or otherwise hauled off.

The best answer, of course, is a tow from another boat but that's not always possible. Lastly, one can wait until the tide floats the boat clear, but only if the grounding occurred at less than full high tide.

Aground on the edge of a shoal (FAR LEFT), this cruising ketch has hoisted all sail and is now waiting for the tide to lift her off.

Running aground (LEFT) is something which may happen eventually even to the best skippers. If conditions are safe, crew members may try climbing out to the end of the boom in an attempt to heel the boat and thereby reduce draft.

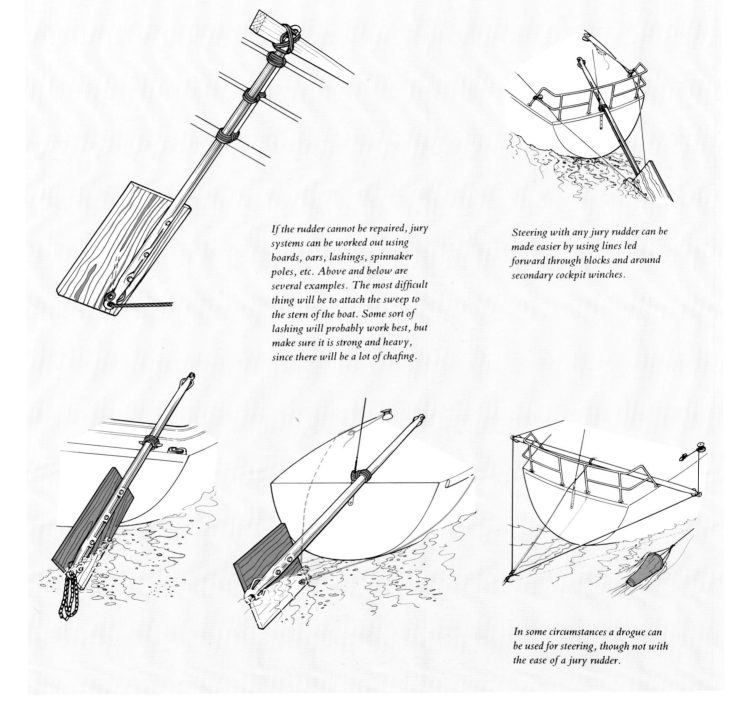

If the rudder cannot be repaired, jury systems can be worked out using boards, oars, lashings, spinnaker poles, etc. Above and below are several examples. The most difficult thing will be to attach the sweep to the stern of the boat. Some sort of lashing will probably work best, but make sure it is strong and heavy, since there will be a lot of chafing.

Steering with any jury rudder can be made easier by using lines led forward through blocks and around secondary cockpit winches.

In some circumstances a drogue can be used for steering, though not with the ease of a jury rudder.

DISMASTING

Sometimes climatic conditions are so ferocious that the mast bends or breaks in one or more places.

If you are dismasted, assess the situation immediately. Be extremely careful as you move about on deck in case you trip over any of the broken mast: the boat will have a much quicker and very different motion now that the damping effect of the rig and mast has gone.

A mast that has gone overboard presents a serious threat to the continuing integrity of the hull, especially in heavy weather. In calm seas, you may be able to hoist the mast back on board. If the mast is sizeable and therefore heavy, a better procedure will be to lash it to the hull. Hoisting will necessitate securing the spar at least three points along its length, and rigging tackles fore, aft

Dismasted during an inshore race.

and amidships – using winches in the cockpit, perhaps the vang to the maststep and the anchor windlass with appropriate jury-rigged fairleads. Be sure that the hull is appropriately fendered.

Normally, it ought to be possible to tie the mast steady. If you are drifting toward danger, do not start the engine until all the loose rope and wire has been secured, otherwise they might jam either the propeller or the rudder, or both. In shallow water, it may be possible to anchor.

If you decide to lash the mast to the side of the boat , a large part of the rigging will have to be cut away. This can be done either by undoing the rigging screws (which will most likely be bent out of shape by the shock) or by cutting the rigging wires, either with cable cutters or with a cold chisel and hammer against a steel block. Be warned: rod rigging will not be so easy to cut. That rigging which can be left – lower shrouds on the side of the vessel on which the mast went over – should be, as added security. Remember, however, that it may be necessary, in increasing heavy weather, to cut the mast adrift. Those remaining attachment points will hamper any efforts to do so.

With luck, the boom can be removed and the remainder of the broken mast lashed aboard. If you are close to port and the engine is serviceable, you may be able to motor to safety. Outside assistance will probably not be necessary unless any of the crew is injured. If you are out at sea and have only limited fuel, you may be forced to build a jury rig when the weather conditions improve.

Breaks at the spreaders are more common than one would wish to imagine. The number of fittings, terminals, etc. at that point can weaken the mast. If the mast should fracture and the upper portion come tumbling down, lash it to deck. If the mast is left dangling, lash the upper part to the portion left standing; trying to cut down the top and maneuver it to the deck can be a tricky and dangerous job.

STEERING FAILURE

The majority of steering failures are caused not by the loss of the rudder blade but by the breakdown of the mechanism controlling it. (Most organizers of coastal races require an emergency tiller to be carried.) On wheel-steered boats for instance, the problem is usually caused simply by the breaking of a link in the wire-chain system or by one of the cables jumping off a sheave. It is a sensible precaution to practice fitting your emergency tiller and seeing how the boat handles. Some tillers supplied as standard by boat builders are far from satisfactory because they either foul deck gear or are so short that lines have to be rigged to them and led to winches to relieve the load.

If the blade itself is lost, first of all check to see that no water is coming in via the rudder stock.

For tiller repair, see pp. 128–129.

Some liferafts have water pockets to provide stability.

Boarding the raft (RIGHT); before abandoning the boat, don as much warm clothing as possible.

If you do go overboard and are wearing a flotation device, the best way to keep warm and alert is to assume a fetal position. Stay this way until you have your wits about you and can assess how best to get back on board or on to a liferaft.

ABANDON SHIP

If the boat is in imminent danger of sinking, the liferaft must be launched but only as a last resort. In the 1979 Fastnet Race lives were lost from the liferafts of boats which ultimately survived the storm.

When launching the raft, it is essential that the painter is made fast to the boat so that the raft does not blow away as soon as it inflates. It is preferable to launch the liferaft to leeward so that there is a modicum of protection when it is boarded. An exception to this is a situation in which you are trying to escape from a fire; being upwind should then help you keep clear of the flames. Any gear to be taken aboard the raft should be tied to a crew-member wearing a lifejacket. Such gear could include flares in a waterproof container, an EPIRB and a 'panic bag' containing, for example, knife, chocolate, survival blanket, food rations and water.

If there is time, bail the raft out first so that the crew can board dry. It might be necessary however to clamber aboard from the sea or even right the liferaft itself first. To do this, stand on the gas bottle pocket and haul the righting lines. At the doorway, there should be a ladder which sinks deep enough to enable you to grab the handle in the opening and pull your torso on to the top of the tube and roll in. Once in, it is probably better to shift your weight opposite the opening to steady the raft. Deploy the drogue as soon as you can because it contributes greatly to the stability of the raft.

SOME POINTS TO CONSIDER WHEN ABANDONING SHIP

If, and only if, the mother ship is in imminent danger of sinking, inflate liferaft *on deck* or by tossing overboard to activate CO_2 cylinders. Do not attempt inflation below or in the cockpit. Make sure raft is tethered before inflating. In very heavy weather the raft may flip. Do not attempt to right it until necessary.

Extra water, food, etc. should be packed at hand in a duffel. Tie it to the raft if possible. Ship's papers, passport, etc. should be in a waterproof pouch, responsibility of the captain. If at all possible, get extra flares, radio emergency beacon and a compass aboard, as well as a chart of the area. All this takes preplanning.

Hypothermia is one of the surest ways to quick death. Keep fully clothed, including hat and boots. Water within the oilskins will have something of a wetsuit effect, and wet clothing, especially if wool, will have a high insulating effect. Move as little as possible, only so much as is necessary to stay afloat. Attempting to swim, no matter how strong a swimmer you are, will result in heat loss on a massive scale, unconsciousness and death.

Leave the raft tethered to the ship. Too many people have been lost attempting to leap from ship to raft. Only when you are aboard should the tether be cut. Take what care you can not to cut the raft also.

If you have no liferaft or dinghy, put on your life-jacket, and enter the water from the windward side of the boat. From any other point the boat can drift down, or back down or slip to windward, endangering anyone in the water. Keep all clothes on, and assume a fetal position to conserve body heat. A light, whistle and knife should be attached to the life vest. Try to stay calm.

Pickup by ship or helicopter is a dangerous, touchy and frightening maneuver. Try to be hoisted aboard, rather than climbing a ladder. Leave the boat from bow or stern and time the move up to coincide with the crest of a wave.

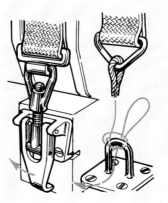

The raft must be kept secure on the deck yet at the same time be capable of being freed with ease. Either of these methods is satisfactory: a patented adjustable catch, or a padeye with light lashings that can be cut with a knife.

C H A P T E R   T H I R T E E N

MEDICAL FACTORS AND FIRST AID

As we have just seen, cold can kill. It is not necessary to fall overboard in order to feel the debilitating effects of cold. Many sailors will have experienced chilly watches and the expression 'feeling the cold in my bones' is very apt. Hypothermia is a decrease in the body's temperature from its regular 98.6° Fahrenheit (37°C).

Prevention is better than cure and a regular supply of hot drinks is beneficial. The ability to operate in the galley efficiently is therefore more important in foul conditions than in fair.

The symptoms of hypothermia are shivering, numbness, cramp and, as the condition deteriorates to critical levels, listlessness, slurred speech and abnormal behaviour. In the very worst cases the pupils dilate, the pulse becomes weak and breathing becomes difficult. Medical attention is imperative.

If these symptoms are detected among your crew, the patient should be gently rewarmed. Tepid drinks should be given but alcohol must be avoided at all costs. It may give a glowing sensation, but by stimulating the heart it merely transmits heat from the core to the surface where it is lost. The patient can be wrapped in a sleeping bag, although another source of heat inside the bag is helpful. The patient must of course be kept dry; evaporation of water on the skin's surface drains away heat.

HYPOTHERMIA

The sun can be as much of a problem to the unwary as the cold. Combine a full day's sailing with the reflective effect of the sea and the result is a great deal more exposure to the sun than is normally experienced ashore. The problem is worsened by the fact that some of the best sailing areas in the world are located beneath a clean atmosphere and thus in strong and intense ultraviolet light.

Ensure that there is a good supply of suntan lotion, including total block. Pay particular attention to those

Adequate clothing is essential for offshore sailing. Not only is hypothermia progressively debilitating physically and mentally, but the cold actively promotes seasickness.

areas which catch the sun most: nose; back of neck; shoulders; thighs; and tops of feet. Waterproof lotion is recommended: the combined effects of sunburn and salt spray is particularly painful.

Keep protected, even on cool days. Drink what you need to feel comfortable. Do NOT ration water. The body can store water and the old saw about rationing has been fairly convincingly disproved by recent US Army Survival School studies. If heatstroke occurs, intensive, rapid cooling is called for. Put victim in cold-water bath (plugged cockpit) or wrap in soaked sheets. Seawater works well. After body temperature has dropped to 102°F (38.9°C), cease cold treatment. Massage arms and legs to promote cooling circulation. As soon as possible start taking cool liquids by mouth. Follow-up medical care is necessary, as potentially serious damage can be inflicted on internal organs.

The eyes must not be forgotten either. Without protection they can become sore, red and watery. Prolonged exposure can actually damage them.

SEASICKNESS

Many sailors, experienced and inexperienced alike, are affected by seasickness. Even the great British Admiral, Lord Nelson, was a chronic sufferer and the only advantage experienced sailors have is the knowledge of how to mitigate its effects.

There are many drugs available on the market, although drowsiness is a common side effect. Recently, drugs which anesthetize the inner ear have been made available as our balance mechanism in the ears' semi-

The crew should always be wary of overexposure to the sun.

circular canals has much to do with controlling motion sickness. Two examples of these drugs are Stugeron, available in England, and Transderm-Scop, increasingly available worldwide. Another drug widely recommended is Bucladin. But patent medicines work or don't work according to the individual. Chronic seasickness must be dealt with as best as one can. Milder forms can often be cured by focusing on a distant horizon, keeping blood sugar levels up, and avoiding interiors or exaggerated sense of motion.

Simpler and more obvious ways to avoid sickness include not consuming excessive amounts of alcohol or rich foods.

Those suffering will often be lethargic, weak and may resist offers of help. If they are ill, they will probably be better kept warm below rather than crouching on deck to leeward. However, some individuals might prefer keeping a firm sight of the horizon. If so, put them in a safety harness and interest them in the running of the boat. A stint at the helm can be recuperative.

The crew will expend a great deal of energy at sea, particularly in cold weather. Plenty of hot food is essential.

MORALE

The greatest concurrent problem with any injury at sea may be fear. Not only take appropriate action but also reassure the injured person. Care, concern and will, can play as important a part as anything to help alleviate distress and aid someone on the path to recovery.

Rest is vital to an enjoyable passage. Note the berth's leecloth.

MEDICAL EMERGENCIES

Besides having a well-stocked first aid kit on board you should also carry a manual, such as that published by the Red Cross organization. If you intend sailing regularly over long distances, then attending training courses is a sensible preparation.

At the very least you should be able to cope with common sailing accidents resulting in cuts, fractures and scalds. If you sail in waters where poisoning from marine life is common you should learn how to deal with this.

Above all, an understanding of emergency resuscitation is vital. Seconds count and there will be no time to thumb frantically through the manual.

If you are sailing with a new crew, find out whether they have any particular ailments. A diabetic, for instance, may need treatment which cannot be delayed until you return ashore.

Certain medical conditions will be beyond your ability to treat. If you are far from shore, you must use your judgement and common sense, and do everything in your power to aid the patient with what you have at hand. Certain infections can be held at bay with antibiotics. Certain fractures can be immobilized until a doctor is at hand. But other conditions may be impossible to do much about. Internal hemorrhaging, heart attack, certain types of poisoning, extreme hypothermia may be beyond anything you can do. You can but try.

BLEEDING

The only pressure point that matters is directly over the bleeding area. Use sterile, soft, absorbent material. Small cuts will usually stop bleeding after a short while; larger cuts should have the material taped over until further action can be taken. Cleanse with soap and water or with hydrogen peroxide. Only use a tourniquet in emergencies for extremely heavy bleeding.

BURNS

For all burns, the immediate treatment is to apply cold water liberally. Use soaked cloths, either fresh or salt water. Avoid running water and ointments, creams or sprays. With anything more than a first-degree burn, cover with sterile petroleum jelly, gauze and a sterile dressing. For second- and third-degree burns, seek immediate medical attention. Life-threatening burns can cause shock and the danger of infection. Take fluids orally, keep dressings in place, take painkillers and antibiotics if more than 24 hours are likely to elapse before a doctor will be able to diagnose the extent of your injuries and give treatment accordingly.

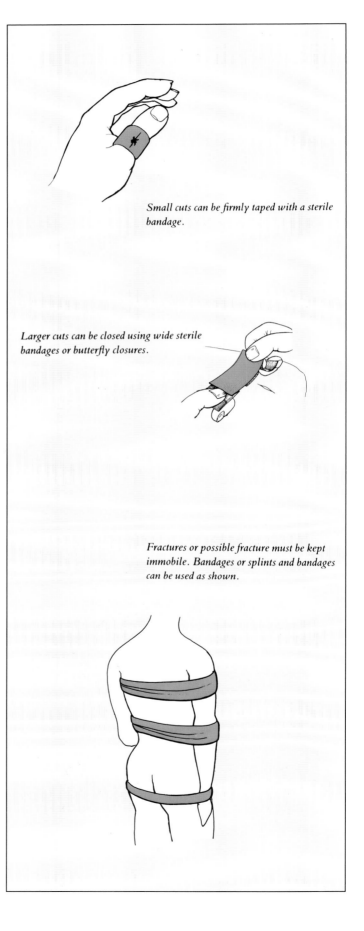

Small cuts can be firmly taped with a sterile bandage.

Larger cuts can be closed using wide sterile bandages or butterfly closures.

Fractures or possible fracture must be kept immobile. Bandages or splints and bandages can be used as shown.

CUTS

Use strip or butterfly bandages to close a cut, apply pressure and keep it clean. Larger cuts will require stitching and prompt medical attention. If signs of infection appear, use antibiotics.

FEVER

Use aspirin (ASA) or paracetamol (acetaminophen), no more than 10 grains every 4 hours. Do NOT increase dosage. Cool sponge baths can aid in reducing fever. Dress lightly unless suffering chills. If fever is high and persists, infection is possible and antibiotics are called for. If no change after 48 hours, seek immediate medical attention.

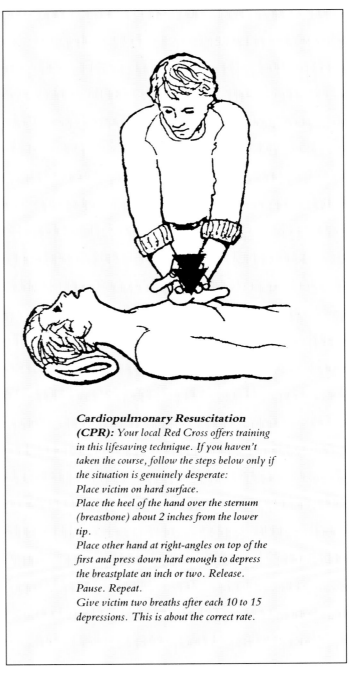

Cardiopulmonary Resuscitation (CPR): *Your local Red Cross offers training in this lifesaving technique. If you haven't taken the course, follow the steps below only if the situation is genuinely desperate:*
Place victim on hard surface.
Place the heel of the hand over the sternum (breastbone) about 2 inches from the lower tip.
Place other hand at right-angles on top of the first and press down hard enough to depress the breastplate an inch or two. Release. Pause. Repeat.
Give victim two breaths after each 10 to 15 depressions. This is about the correct rate.

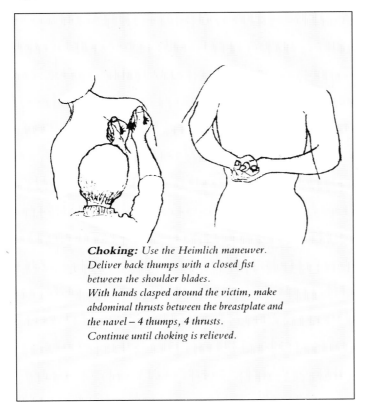

Choking: *Use the Heimlich maneuver.*
Deliver back thumps with a closed fist between the shoulder blades.
With hands clasped around the victim, make abdominal thrusts between the breastplate and the navel – 4 thumps, 4 thrusts.
Continue until choking is relieved.

FRACTURES

Immobilize immediately. Apply ice packs if possible. Give pain medication. Do NOT try to set the fracture, merely keep it from moving with splints or bandages. Keep tight enough but not so tight as to stop or hinder circulation. Seek medical aid immediately. Compound fractures – where skin has been broken – will require cleansing of the wound and antibiotics. Be prepared also to treat for shock, including possible drowsiness, confusion or loss of consciousness (see paragraph immediate right).

SHOCK

Shock can follow any severe injury, particularly serious burns or blood loss. It is an indication of internal bleeding. The victim will be pale, faint and sweaty with a weak, rapid pulse and cold, moist skin. He may be thirsty, drowsy and confused; he will eventually lose consciousness. Shock is fatal unless treated, yet there is little one can do without medical facilities. *Summon help immediately!* Lay the victim on his back and raise the legs about 1ft (30cm) with cushions or the like. Keep the victim warm.

CHAPTER FOURTEEN

MAINTENANCE AND REPAIRS

MAINTAINING THE BOTTOM

The job of maintaining a good finish on the bottom is an important one for two reasons: firstly a smooth finish can improve a boat's speed and efficiency; and secondly an effective paint job with a high-quality *antifouling* paint can help keep marine growth (algae, weeds, barnacles) off the surface.

Most boats kept in salt water rely on a basic oil-based copper-filled paint, applied at the start of each season.

Do read the instructions on the paint tin to determine how soon a boat must be launched after painting. Most common bottom paints must touch seawater within two or three days from application, while some new types can go 60 days or longer.

It is best to paint the *boot-top* (the narrow band just above the waterline) before finishing the bottom, as painting the bottom *up* to the stripe is usually easier than painting the stripe *down* to edge against the bottom paint. Use 'enamel-type' antifouling paint on your boot-top.

On some boats, bottom paint may have flaked away from the ballast of the keel. If that material is exposed, it should be primed before applying bottom paint. There are many materials made for this purpose, and it's wise to consult your chandlery for the best available for your purpose.

All boats have small zinc plates bolted to the bottom to help ward off the destructive action of electrolysis. The zinc plates on your boat should look worn and eaten away, showing that the zincs are being electrolyzed instead of allowing your boat's other underwater metals to succumb to the destructive process. Replace any worn zincs with new ones.

Note: *Never paint your zincs; the coating would prevent them from contacting the water as they should.*

MAINTAINING THE TOPSIDES

The sides of your boat's hull above the waterline are called *topsides*. Most fiberglass boats have a hard coating of polymerized resin on the topsides, called *gel-coat*.

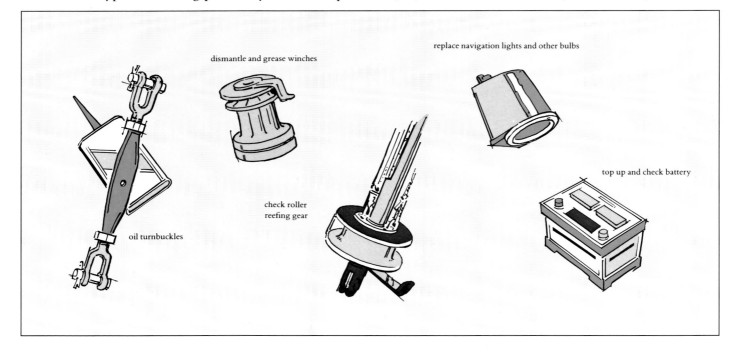

dismantle and grease winches

replace navigation lights and other bulbs

oil turnbuckles

check roller reefing gear

top up and check battery

Gel-coat requires little maintenance. It needs wax each year to help resist fading, and it should be repaired when it is scratched or damaged.

To repair a surface blemish in gel-coat, use a kit designed for the purpose. Most chandlers carry them. It is important to watch the temperature on the day of application, and make sure it is within the specifications of the manufacturer. Most gel-coat repair kits allow the applicator to grind and/or polish shortly after drying.

There may come a time when painting is the only way to renew a boat's topside finish. This is always true on a wooden boat, where yearly painting is usual, but even fiberglass boats need to be painted – especially when their gel-coat fades and dulls.

On both wooden and fibreglass boats, a process of sanding and filling is required to gain a smooth, even surface for painting. The materials and methods for sanding and filling vary and so it's wise for the beginner to consult instructional guides on the subject, or to inquire of the yard's expert personnel.

Once the hull is fair, the choice of paint is up to the owner. There are three major classes of topside paints:

(1) Alkyd enamel – normal oil-based paint, designed to hold up through one season's use in normal weather conditions. Does not necessarily need special primers. (Least expensive.)

(2) One-part polyurethane – high-gloss polyurethane-based paint designed to last perhaps two or three seasons. Must be applied over special primers. (Mid-priced.)

(3) Two-part polyurethane – an extremely high-gloss coating designed to last from three to five years. Must be applied over special primers and surfacing materials, and is usually recommended for professional application. (Most expensive.)

The last two systems are most often used on fiberglass boats, as they show superior adhesion to the prepared gel-coat. Both can be touched up, though with some difficulty.

Alkyd enamel is usually used on wooden boats, as swelling and shrinkage of planking and moisture retention in wood usually do more to deteriorate surface paint than normal weathering, and painting therefore must be done annually.

MAINTAINING THE BRIGHTWORK

Often, some wood on a boat is left unpainted – natural. This *brightwork* must be treated with preservative or sealant, or eventually it will suffer the ravages of salt water and sun.

Oil There are numerous types of oil available with which an owner may coat his brightwork. Teak is especially common on newer boats, and this wood is perfectly suited to oiling.

Fitting out – a time to renew and repair is made considerably easier with a generator and power tools.

When oiling teak, make sure to rub small amounts of oil in thoroughly with a terrycloth rag. Doing this frequently (about once a month) will keep the teak rich-looking and well sealed

Varnish Varnish is another sealant, but has properties that make it more permanent. However, because teak usually has natural oils present in its grain, it is one wood that should not be varnished.

Varnish dries into a hard, glossy surface. Unlike oils, it must be built-up coat after coat, with the varnisher making sure to sand lightly between coats. A good varnish job can last a long time, with a simple touch-up (a light coat or two) all that's required each year.

Varnish works well on seasoned oak, softwoods, and on mahogany.

Note that there are many types of varnish, from the traditional spar varnish to the new hi-tech clear polyurethanes. Ask your chandler for his recommendations.

RIG MAINTENANCE

Since the rig must support all your sails and absorb all the stresses of sailing throughout the season, it's important to examine it thoroughly at the beginning of the season each year.

Mast On an aluminium mast, check all mast-mounted fittings and tangs. Make sure there is no cracking of the extrusion around tangs and bolts, and make sure that none of the stainless fittings are showing signs of cracking around their fastenings.

On a wood mast, do all the above, but also check for cracks and separations in any glue lines, and cracks or gaps in mounting blocks and at the mast's butt. Refinish the mast as appropriate each year.

Check all mast wiring by examining carefully for deterioration in the wire casing, and set up a battery to test the masthead light, spreader lights, and any other mast-mounted lights. Replace any worn wiring.

Oil masthead main-halyard sheave, and replace pin and/or sheave if worn.

Examine and oil or replace (if necessary) any other blocks – spinnaker, jib, topping lift(s), etc.

Standing rigging Examine closely the swaged terminals on all wire. Look for small cracks at the swaged collars, and have the entire shroud or stay replaced if swages show signs of bad cracking.

Look for elongated clevis holes on all swaged ends, as well as on any other terminal end. Elongation reflects serious strain and distortion of the alloy.

Check wire and terminals for signs of rust. Rust could indicate a developing problem. Clean it away and examine closely for cracking at terminal.

Examine turnbuckles for stretching or elongation at clevis holes and threads. Check holes and body for cracking damage. Replace whole unit if necessary. Lubricate threads with moisture-penetrating lubricant. Make sure cotter pins are inserted in clevises of correct size for terminals and turnbuckles in rig when set up.

Running rigging Make sure all blocks are lubricated with moisture-penetrating lubricant, or with anhydrous lanolin. Check that all fittings requiring cotter pins have fresh ones.

Make sure swivels and blocks are without too much play. If axles or swivel pins seem worn, replace.

Check all line for chafe and wear. Repair any unravelling, and replace any questionable line.

Lubricate all winches according to manufacturer's instructions. Make sure that boom, spinnaker pole, and any other spars are examined as thoroughly as the mast.

Lubricate and check any roller-furling gear. Check furling pendant for unravelling and signs of wear.

Check all wire halyards for burrs, and replace if flattened or pinched at any point.

The masthead and standing rigging should not be neglected. A mid-season check by bosun's chair will ensure that masthead fittings and shackles have not worked loose nor standing rigging frayed at the terminals or swages.

ONGOING GENERAL MAINTENANCE

There are many things that must be attended to on an ongoing basis as well as the ship's power-plant and support systems.

Decks If teak, keep scrubbed. Oiling teak decks is all right, but too much oil will make them slippery when wet.

If fiberglass, keep clean.

If canvas-covered wood, keep painted, using porch-and-deck enamel if possible, as it flexes more than marine paint. Keep canvas sealed, especially at edges; and replace canvas if it begins to tear and/or deteriorate.

If leaking develops, search for source(s). When found, mark source and attack when dry with surface sealers. Check with local chandler on best material for purpose.

Ship's electrical system Maintain good check on battery charge. Keep all external light fixtures well sealed from moisture. Keep all internal wiring terminals, switches, and busses sprayed with moisture-penetrating lubricant.

Bilges Keep bilges as clean as possible. Clean bilge pump intake screen frequently. Use oil-absorptive sponge or emulsifier to disperse and absorb stray oil.

Lockers Keep stowage spaces dry and clean. Keep dry food stores enclosed and sealed in plastic containers. Bars of fragrant soap placed in each locker space help keep boat 'sweet' smelling without overdoing it. In winter season, keep mildew-absorptive bags aboard.

Underwater If possible, scrub the boat's bottom once in the middle of the season. Also, make sure the propeller remains free of barnacles.

As you can see, maintenance is an ongoing fact of life on a boat. In fact, to a beginner it may seem as though a lot of hard work, and some considerable expense, is involved with only a tenuous promise of reward. But it can be one of the more enjoyable parts of your life under sail.

Use your good common sense about every aspect of your boat's many systems. Ask the advice of your yard and of friends you respect. Read more about the specifics you're concerned with. Through the years, you will develop your skills and insights until you become a fine seaman. And when you do, you can pass along what you've learned.

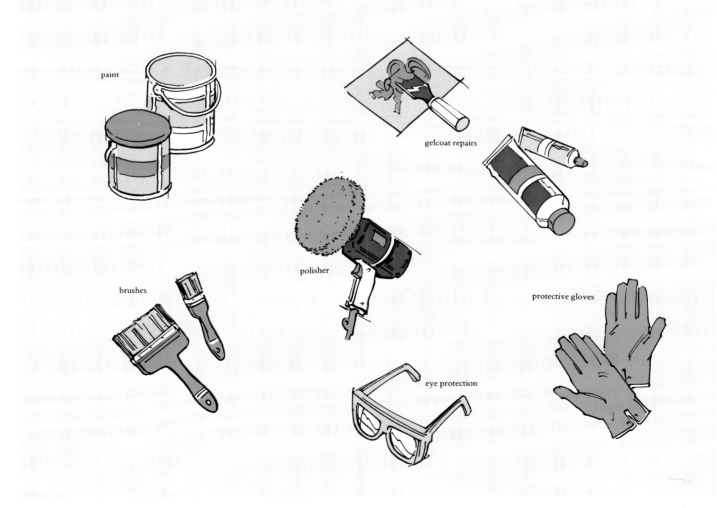

paint

gelcoat repairs

polisher

brushes

protective gloves

eye protection

REPAIRS: RIGGING A JURY MAST

When making a jury rig it will be easier if the top part of the mast with its sheaves and shroud attachment points can be used. If the original mast was keel-stepped it is likely that a stump will remain to which the section of mast can be lashed. If, however, there is no such stump, a means will have to be found to raise the section of mast into an upright position. One method is to use the boom or spinnaker pole as a bi-pod to create greater leverage on a rope raising the section. Jury rigging needs to be attached before the section is raised and if it is rope and not wire it can be tensioned more easily.

It may be possible to set a deep-reefed mainsail or two small headsails. You will not be able to steer much closer to the wind than 60° to seek a destination downwind.

There have been some remarkable achievements under jury rig. Solo sailors dismasted in mid-Atlantic have reached their original destination, while the yacht *Ceramco New Zealand* logged 16 knots in this condition when she broke her mast during the first leg of the 1981/2 Whitbread Round the World Race.

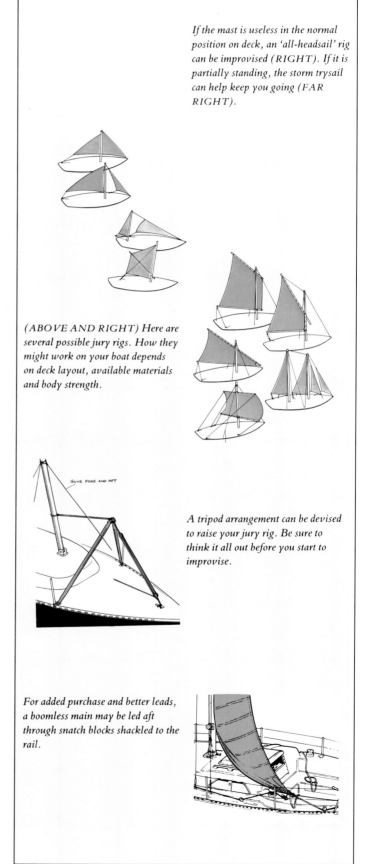

If the mast is useless in the normal position on deck, an 'all-headsail' rig can be improvised (RIGHT). If it is partially standing, the storm trysail can help keep you going (FAR RIGHT).

(ABOVE AND RIGHT) Here are several possible jury rigs. How they might work on your boat depends on deck layout, available materials and body strength.

GUYS FORE AND AFT

A tripod arrangement can be devised to raise your jury rig. Be sure to think it all out before you start to improvise.

For added purchase and better leads, a boomless main may be led aft through snatch blocks shackled to the rail.

If you find yourself grounded on a shelving patch (ABOVE), you may be able to haul off by rowing out a kedge into deeper water, then winching the boat off the bottom. Always sound the surrounding water first – otherwise, you may find you have dragged your vessel firmer on to the hard!

Splints for repairing a broken boom (RIGHT) can be fashioned from fiddle rails, floorboards, an oar or spare sail battens. If your mainsail foot slides into a grooved boom, it may be reset flying, with only the clew attached to the outhaul fitting.

SOME POINTS TO CONSIDER WHEN RIGGING A JURY MAST

Depending upon the damage inflicted to the mast, a jury rig may be an addition to what remains standing or it may be an entire make-do structure. If the mast has broken above the spreaders, the storm trysail may work as a mainsail with only a forestay and backstay pieced together from spare wire and wire rope clips. If only the mizzen remains, a forestay can be fashioned – albeit at a very low angle – and a jib can be modified to be set flying from said stay. As long as the remaining bit of mast has retained the lower shrouds, a low-efficiency sailing rig is not only possible but relatively simple to fabricate.

If the mast breaks at or near deck level, a different set of criteria apply. First see what is salvageable from the leavings of your once noble spar. It may be possible to save stays, hardware or a section of the spar itself. Before you decide what you will do, see what you have to work with.

Having made an inventory of working materials – not forgetting oars, spinnaker and jockey poles, bunk fronts, etc. – sit below with a clean sheet of paper, some basic measurements (base of foretriangle, length of longest usable mast section, length of various salvaged wire, etc.) and a pencil and see what *might* be possible. Perhaps the most important thing to remember is that the rig you design must be able to be created, hoisted and used by the available manpower and the available skills. If you are within sight of land, turn on the engine!

Having come up with a solution, collect and assemble all the necessary parts. Do as much as possible with the new rig *on deck*. The less needed to be done aloft, the safer.

Setting sail may mean adopting some odd and backended configurations. Jibs may be turned on end, or sewn together. Storm sails may be the best driving sails for a reduced rig, and setting them flying may be the best, and safest, means of propulsion. What is most important is to devise a sail combination that will get you where you wish tö go. Quite often sprit-sails, lateen rigs, makeshift schooners and square sails will serve the purpose quite well.

RIGGING A JURY BOOM

Use flat-sided splints – floorboards, fiddles, bunk boards – lashed to either side of the boom extending a couple of feet beyond the break either side.

If the boom is shattered or fractured beyond repair, remove it and lash a spinnaker pole, boat hook or such to the gooseneck, with the mainsail reefed. Tie reef points around the jury boom.

If the gooseneck ruptures, lash the inboard end of the boom to the mast using reefing hooks or any projection. Apply chafe protection.

If all else fails, and you must sail without a boom, reinforce the clew and lead separate sheets to the quarters, then forward to winches by way of the spinnaker turning blocks; or, in desperation, bend sheets to the clew fitting, lash around the clew corner and lead as above.

Storm trysails are remarkably efficient, rarely used sails. You should, of course, know how to set one, and have it in readiness and good repair with its sheets attached. Since it is designed to be used boomless, you have, in your sail locker, the perfect solution to a broken boom.

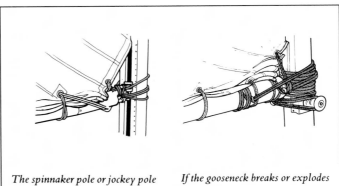

The spinnaker pole or jockey pole may be used if the boom is beyond repair (ABOVE). Lash the end securely with ⅜in (8mm) line.

If the gooseneck breaks or explodes (it can happen), use reefing hooks or a cringle attachment shackle to lash the boom to the mast (ABOVE).

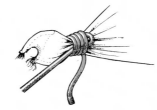

If no jury boom can be rigged, lash the clew of the mainsail securely and lead sheets to each quarter (ABOVE), much as you would rig a storm trysail.

ROPEWORK

Ropework is a way of life for the sailor, day in and day out. Its maintenance, repair, and replacement are the bread and butter of his routine.

For the inshore sailor, the relatively small demands of shipboard seamanship dictate a less evolved, simpler level of marlinspike skill. Some elementary knots and the basics of fibre rope splicing are all that one needs to manage a small cruising boat in protected waters.

Learn these; they are the basics from which you will build a more complete body of skill.

FIGURE OF EIGHT

This knot is used to stop a rope slipping through an eye or block. It is equally simple to tie and undo.

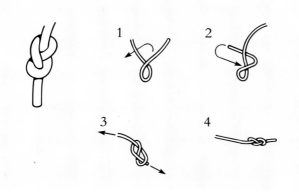

REEF KNOT

Originally used to tie reefing lines, the reef knot is formed from two half hitches. To untie a reef knot (7 and 8), hold one end of the rope in one hand and the 'standing' part in the other and 'push' the knot off.

SHEET BEND

This knot can be used to join together two ropes of unequal thickness or to fasten a line to an eye. It is easily undone by bending it in the center and pushing the bight down on the half hitch.

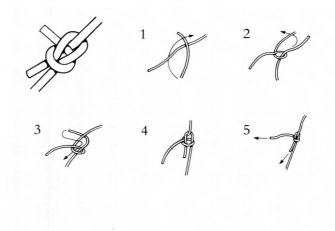

ROUND TURN AND TWO HALF HITCHES

Widely used to secure a heavy load to a spar, ring or any standing object. The rope can be secured with two half hitches.

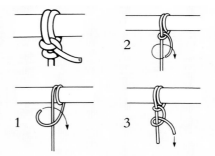

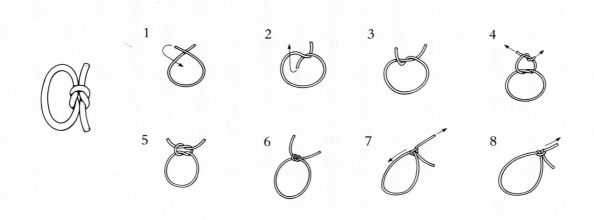

CLOVE HITCH

Particularly useful for temporarily tying small items. However, the knot only holds well when under constant strain at right-angles to the standing object.

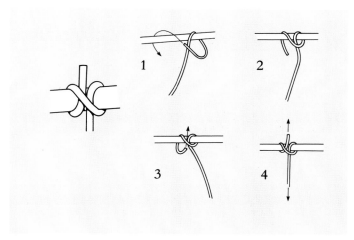

WHIPPING

A method of finishing the ends of rope with twine to prevent them from unravelling.

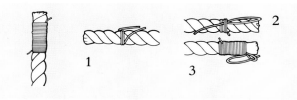

BOWLINE

A simple knot for forming an eye at the end of a rope.

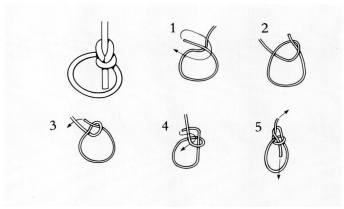

EYE SPLICE

Used to form a fixed loop at the end of a rope. It is much stronger than any knot.

1 Form required eye. Tuck middle strand under one strand of standing part. Tuck second strand of end part over next strand of standing part and pull tight.

2 Flop splice. Tuck last full strand under remaining strand. Pull tight.

3 Continue tucking each strand alternately going over and under strands in standing part. Pull tight after each tuck.

4 After five tucks are completed, cut off loose ends.

ROLLING HITCH

This knot is used to tie a rope to a spar when the strain on the knot is parallel to the object to which it is tied.

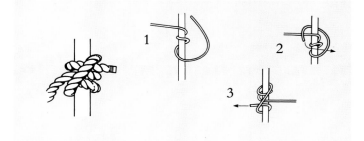

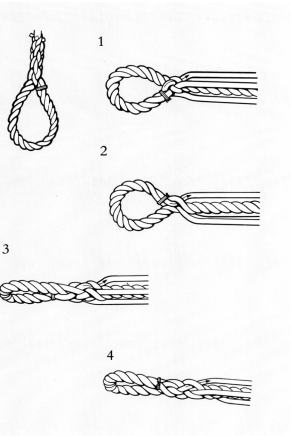

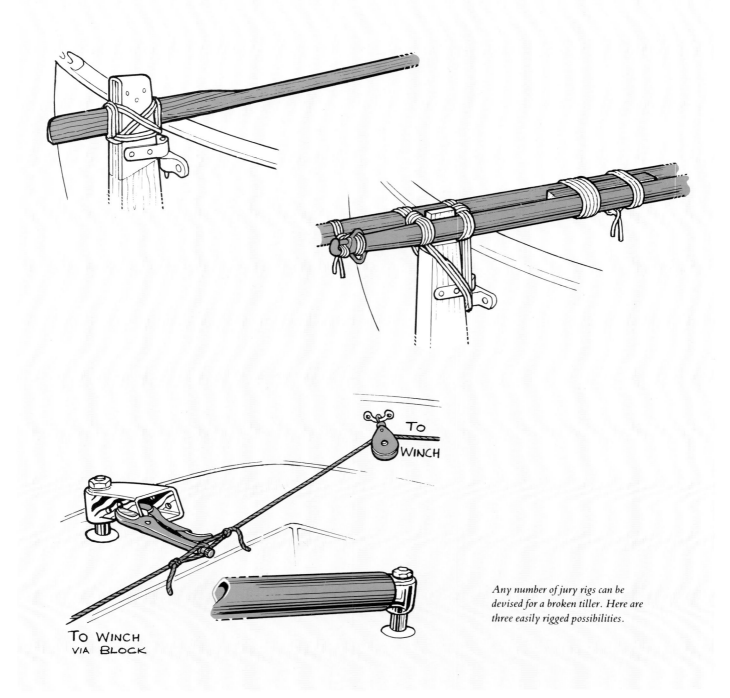

Any number of jury rigs can be devised for a broken tiller. Here are three easily rigged possibilities.

TO WINCH

TO WINCH
VIA BLOCK

RUNNING REPAIRS TO THE RIGGING

It is possible for part of the standing rigging to be damaged without losing the mast. However, swift action is required to take as much pressure as possible off the damaged area. For example, if a windward shroud fails, go about on to the opposite tack; if the forestay fails, bear away immediately; and if the backstay fails steer upwind and sheet in the mainsail. Try to take sea state into account, as undue pitching and rolling can cause almost as much damage as the original fitting's initially letting go.

It is often possible to take a spare halyard or the topping lift out to a strong point on the deck and tension it as a substitute. Your most useful equipment for jury rigging, besides a spare halyard, will be wire rope and bulldog clips or C-clamps. These should be galvanized, not stainless steel, which has a tendency to slip.

REPAIRS TO THE STEERING GEAR

A broken tiller is surprisingly difficult to replace as there are few suitable pieces of timber aboard and there is often a special fitting joining tiller to the head of the rudder. It makes sense, therefore, to carry a spare for both. It is also a sensible precaution to practice fitting your emergency tiller and see how the boat handles.

If wind vane auto-steering is fitted it may be possible to use its servo rudder once the sail area is suitably reduced.

Some form of emergency steering may sometimes have to be rigged. Control can often be achieved by playing with sail trim: sheeting in the mainsail to bring the boat into the wind; sheeting in the headsail to bring the bow away from the wind. The effect might be enhanced by setting a jib on the backstay instead of using the mainsail, or by towing a drogue or bucket. For a jury rudder you will need to use the spinnaker or jib pole over the transom. On the outboard end attach a floorboard, locker top or something similar (this may be pre-drilled for just such an eventuality). The inboard end will need control lines led to blocks on either gunwale and then to a winch. The pole should then pivot about a fulcrum created by lashing the pole to the backstay fitting, or a leg of the aft pulpit, so as to form a crude but effective rudder.

For other steerage problems, see also **Steering failure** on page 113.

REPAIRING HULL DAMAGE

If the hull has been punctured good access through floorboards and lockers is vital. There are various ways to fill the hole and if you are able to pump the water out faster than it is coming in, there is a chance of reaching safety. It may be possible to heel the boat far enough to bring the hull clear of the water. You may be able to place a sail over the hole and secure it around the hull. If the hull curvature is not too extreme, try screwing a piece of plywood over the hole with self-tapping screws or perhaps shoring it in position with other floorboards. Other means of blocking large holes are with sailbags and bunk cushions, while small cracks, such as those around the keel caused by running aground, can be treated with epoxy paste. Most chandlers sell a variety which will set underwater.

There is a growing trend among builders of small to medium-sized boats to make them 'unsinkable'. This entails filling spaces between hull skins with positive buoyancy foam. Tests have shown such boats will be awash, but not sink.

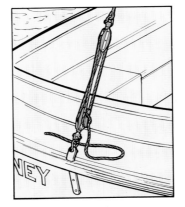

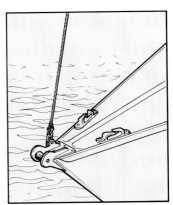

A vang or tackle arrangement can be used to repair a broken backstay, often with a spare halyard led aft.

Likewise, a spare or spinnaker halyard can double as a temporary headstay.

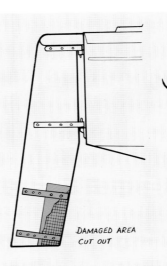

DAMAGED AREA CUT OUT

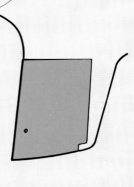

If your rudder breaks only partially, you may be able to patch it with strapping and sheet metal or wood. The key is to make sure that the repaired rudder will be close to the depth of the original.

Plan ahead as much as possible. You could have a pre-drilled hole in the rudder blade. Should you then lose the tiller, a line can be rigged to the cockpit to allow steering by means of blocks and lines.

SOME POINTS TO CONSIDER SHOULD THE TILLER BREAK

Outboard rudder: jam a section of boathook or an oar between the rudder cheeks and lash in place.

Outboard rudder: if tiller fits to either side of rudder blade, lash poles or scrap wood around blade top.

Inboard rudder: cheek-type fitting, like first suggestion above.

Inboard rudder: socket fitting, opening may not be clearable. Use visegrip/molegrip pliers with lines led to coaming blocks and then to winches.

C H A P T E R   F I F T E E N

ENGINES AND POWER-PLANTS

A good engine helps when navigating in close quarters or during times when the situation calls for quick dousing of sail and a dash for that protected cover. Nothing beats that power when the wind dies and you're still a long way from home.

A thorough understanding of handling under power is vital for the beginner because most of the trickier maneuvers will be carried out in this way as confidence is gained in boat-handling. Modern boats handle exceptionally well under power and there is not much to be gained by tackling close quarters situations under sail.

Some boats have diesel engines, others have gasoline engines. Gasoline is a more volatile fuel, requires care in handling, and its storage is often subject to stringent regulation. Diesel fuel, on the other hand, is akin to home heating oil and is quite safe and non-explosive.

However, gasoline engines have had lower selling prices – while diesels have always been rather expensive, though somewhat less so to operate than gas engines.

Today, most engines are small efficient diesels with enough power to move the boat at her theoretical maximum speed in flat water and to punch against a foul tide and/or a head sea in unfavorable conditions. This power, combined with the current practice of short

keels and separate rudders, allows the modern boat to turn in its own length and accelerate and stop with ease, something which could never be said about the old generation of long-keeled yachts.

Diesel engines are now smaller, lighter and more powerful than ever before. Their reliability is commendable, given the hostile environment in which they operate and engine makers are now making greater efforts to mount service points such as pumps, dipsticks and filters at the front of the engine to make maintenance easier.

A typical engine will be sited in an enclosed space under the cockpit companionway area, preferably insulated with sound-absorbent material. To give the engine ventilation, ducting will draw air in from outside, preferably assisted by a spark-proof fan. Fuel is brought from the remote tank, often by copper piping and wire-cased flexible hosing. There should be a stopvalve on the tank which in turn needs to be electrically grounded against static electricity. Because marine fuel is often dirty a filter must be fitted for debris and a water trap for condensate.

Raw sea water is drawn in either to cool the engine directly itself or the intercooler which has a recirculating fresh water cooling system. Seacocks are fitted to both

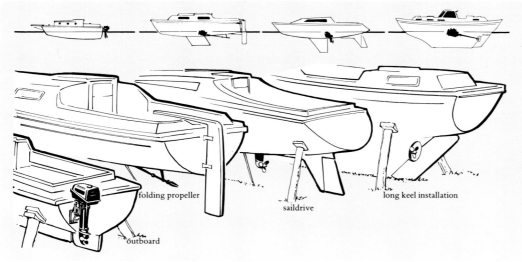

folding propeller

saildrive

long keel installation

outboard

Installation variations for outboard and inboard engines. While the outboard variation is simpler to maintain, it can be vulnerable to damage. Inboard systems, although harder to service, are more reliable.

inlet and outlet. The exhaust is vented to the outside. Sometimes cooling water is added to help silence and cool the exhaust and a water trap is fitted to the system to prevent such water running back to the engine when the yacht heels.

THE EFFECT OF PROPELLERS

Propellers in water work in just the same way as their counterparts do in air; their foil-shaped blades create lift. Generally the slower the speed of the shaft the larger the blades can be. Compare the relatively slow-turning two-bladed propeller fitted to a yacht auxiliary engine to the fast-turning three-bladed propeller found on a high power outboard engine. Reduction gearboxes are often fitted to inboard engines for this reason.

Having the right propeller is important for getting maximum drive, especially as engine performance can be reduced by factors such as friction losses, power take-off for alternators, low energy-value fuel or high operating temperatures.

For the sailing yacht, there is a complicated trade-off between drag and efficiency. Cruising boats will have large fixed two- or three-bladed propellers. Racing yachts will have two-bladed propellers which either fold closed or feather in line with the water flow.

Perhaps the ideal solution is a controllable-pitch feathering propeller. Drag is reduced while sailing and when the engine is used, the propeller pitch can be matched to the engine revs to give maximum speed and economy. Such propellers are, however, more expensive.

The propeller has a marked effect on the handling of the boat because of the propeller or 'paddlewheel' effect. Here the propeller literally paddles the vessel in the direction of its rotation. Hence a clockwise or right-handed propeller (when viewed from astern) will move the boat to the right while a counterclockwise, or left-handed propeller will move the vessel to the left.

For this reason, most boats have a tighter turning circle one way than the other. A right-handed propeller will move the stern to starboard, swing the bows to port and tighten the turn in that direction.
so much so that some boats may be unable to steer 'against' the propeller. The answer here, is to give a burst of power to get the boat moving astern and then back off the power so allowing the rudder to work unhindered.

GENERAL MAINTENANCE TIPS

There are specific items of maintenance every skipper can see to that will help ensure efficiency and longevity from his machinery.

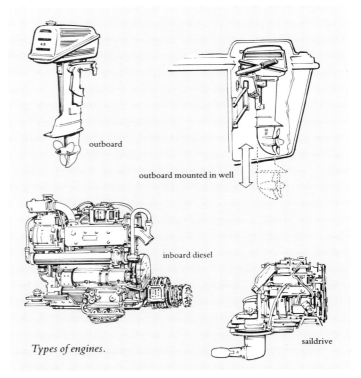

outboard

outboard mounted in well

inboard diesel

saildrive

Types of engines.

Fuel should be kept fresh. Outboard oil/gasoline pre-mixture should be maintained according to manufacturer's specifications. Diesel fuel should pass through a filter/water-separator before passing into the injection system. Gasoline (outboard or inboard) should pass through at least a basic particulate filter before intake.

Note that filter elements should be checked and/or changed frequently and the settling bowl in a water separator should be watched for any signs of the collection of water.

Make sure your spark-plugs are fresh each year. And have the ignition system timed and/or its integrated circuitry inspected and replaced as recommended.

Too much smoke, either from a diesel engine or a petrol engine, can mean excessive combustion of oil, dirty fuel, insufficient air, or any of these.

To keep a running check on all aspects of your propulsion system, maintain an engine log. Listing dates of oil change, coolant top-off, transmission oil change, ignition work, and other maintenance can help remind you when the routine chores are due.

Further, you will want to keep a record of the rpm you run your engine at while cruising, and the amount of fuel you burn at normal levels of operation. Add to those figures the speeds you are able to make good at cruising speed, and you will be able to track your boat's performance.

Not only is this a good thing from a maintenance standpoint, but it will help you to estimate and log speeds for your dead reckoning plots.

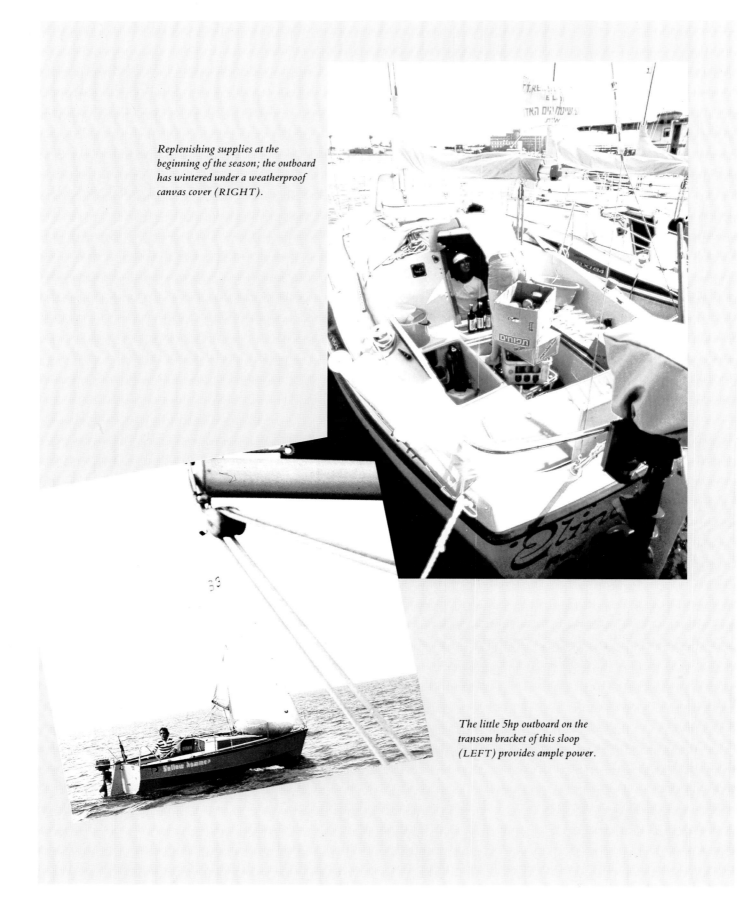

Replenishing supplies at the beginning of the season; the outboard has wintered under a weatherproof canvas cover (RIGHT).

The little 5hp outboard on the transom bracket of this sloop (LEFT) provides ample power.

THE OUTBOARD MOTOR

While inboard engines are common in boats over 25ft (8m), outboard engines offer a cheap alternative below that length and are much cheaper to buy and easier to maintain.

They do use more fuel however; often a smelly two-stroke oil/gasoline mixture. Again, engine manufacturers have improved outboards for sailboats – four-stroke engines and special lower-revving units are available, turning a much coarser-bladed propeller, which is more suitable to the task of pushing a boat along as opposed to a small, light day boat. Controls are front-mounted, and a particularly useful option is a power take-off and battery charging facility.

Many small boats mount their outboards on a sliding/hingeing bracket on the transom. This is far from satisfactory; the engine lifts clear of the water in a sea or with the crew on the foredeck; it requires awkward leaning and lifting over the transom; fuel caps and engine cowlings can be accidentally dropped.

Much better are those which drive the boat through an opening in the hull surrounded by a well, especially if all the controls are close by the helm.

The engine itself, or *powerhead*, is mounted with its *crankshaft* in the vertical plane, and is usually shrouded under a lightweight hood. From the crankshaft, a protected vertical shaft descends to the engine's *lower gearcase*, where power is transmitted at right-angles to the *propeller shaft*, a short shaft that exits the lower gearcase to turn the propeller. If the outboard has any gearshift mechanism at all (some don't), it will be a simple *dog-clutch* mechanism designed to actuate two sets of gears inside the lower gearcase.

Too much power brings no benefit whatsoever. It merely uses more fuel and a large outboard perched on the end of a small dinghy can cause instability. There are some very eager, small, lightweight engines available today producing up to 3.5hp from one cylinder, and offering easy starting. Full gear shift is not necessary for a tender engine.

Because such engines work so close to the water, they should be carefully serviced according to manufacturers' instructions; treat them regularly with WD40, or an equivalent, and if they are stowed on a bracket on the boat's stern rail, be sure to protect them with a neat canvas cover.

In outboards, cooling is relatively simple. All outboards pull seawater through intakes on the lower unit, pump it via a small impeller pump up water channels and into the cooling passages of the aluminum power-head and push it back to sea through both an exhaust-dump and a small passage at the rear of the power-head.

On an outboard motor, check the heavy-grade gear oil in the lower unit for water contamination. Any traces of milkiness indicates seawater slipping past the water pump shaft seal. Many outboards can operate perfectly well with some water in the gear oil, but it is wise to change the oil at least once a season, and replace the seal as recommended by the manufacturer.

Note that outboards typically produce more smoke than inboards, but it is characteristically blue-ish when the engine is running properly.

An outboard engine mounted on the transom (BELOW LEFT).
A long shaft outboard (5hp) (BELOW), suitable for the 16 to 22ft (5 to 7m) boat.

A modern auxiliary under the cockpit (TOP), well sound-proofed and with adequate servicing access.

Don't expect the propeller on a long-keeled cruiser (ABOVE) to give precise handling, especially astern.

THE INBOARD MOTOR

The inboard is usually mounted to hull framing below-decks and deep inside the hull, on the fore and aft center-line of the boat. It is usually made of cast-iron, and may be deisel- or gas-fuelled. The engine is not unlike that in a car. Its horizontally disposed crankshaft is mated to a transmission usually designed to change gears via a hydraulically activated clutch assembly. From the gear-box, power is transmitted via the *propeller shaft* through a watertight seal called a *stuffing box* to the propeller. This can be water- or grease-lubricated. The engine can be mounted back-to-front and the drive arranged in a Vee formation.

The most novel and space-efficient system is the sail-drive, developed by Volvo of Sweden 10 years ago and widely copied since. Here the engine is mounted in its own beds glassed into the hull (as opposed to being fitted to the boat's structure via flexible mountings) and the drive passes through a neoprene membrane in the hull to an outboard-style leg. Such a system is very compact and does away with the need for careful align-ment of shaft, sterngear and engine. Fears about mem-brane failure have so far proved groundless and other engine builders, such as Bukh of Denmark, fit a double membrane with a water alarm in between.

A single lever usually controls the ahead-neutral-astern gearshift and throttle in one arc of movement. Such levers should be within easy reach, yet shielded against accidental snagging by feet or oilskin trousers. Larger boats with wheel steering can have the engine controls mounted on the steering pedestal – a real convenience.

In sight should be an engine rev counter, fuel gauge and water temperature gauge/alarm. The latter gives early warning of a blocked engine-cooling water intake. It is also most helpful if the engine can be started up and shut down from the cockpit: the engine may be required in an instant.

Marine inboard engines are usually cooled with water that is pumped through a set of passages cast-in to the engine block. The water circulates in one of two ways:

(1) Open (raw-water) system This system takes water from the outside of the boat, through a valved hull fitting, and through a strainer before pumping directly into the engine's cooling system. Once the water cools the engine block, it·is dumped into the exhaust system behind the engine itself, where the force of escaping gases pushes it through the silencer (muffler) anῠ out through the exhaust fitting and astern.

(2) Close (fresh-water) system. This system brings water through a hull fitting, strains it, then pumps it through a *heat exchanger*, where it passes over and around a set of copper tubes through which pumps the engine's

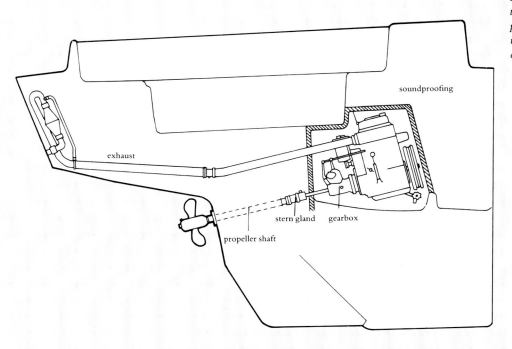

A typical diesel installation showing the looped exhaust system which prevents water from running back into the cylinders. Cooling water often exits via the exhaust system.

soundproofing

exhaust

stern gland   gearbox

propeller shaft

coolant (usually glycol-based antifreeze). The seawater draws the heat out of the antifreeze just the way your car's radiator draws heat. The antifreeze continues to circulate through the engine and heat exchanger, maintaining an even operating temperature. The seawater dumps into the exhaust behind the engine, and is evacuated with exhaust pressure.

Note that the exhaust of an inboard engine must be *high-looped* to raise it above the boat's waterline and break any backflow that could develop because of the relatively low position of the engine. Also note that some method of breaking the potentially dangerous syphon that could develop because of the below-the-water water intake must be provided (usually a vent). Unless the high-loop and syphon-blocking measures are taken, any water either pushed by wave action or syphoned back to the engine through the exhaust could find its way into the cylinders through open exhaust valves and cause severe damage.

Make sure your engine's lubrication system is kept clean. Oil breakdown can lead to rapid wear of piston rings and valves, which in turn can lead to loss of compression. At each oil change (the interval for which is recommended by the manufacturer), change the oil filter.

Make sure your instrument panel is equipped with an oil-pressure gauge and alarm system.

An engine's compression can be checked using a *compression gauge*, checking each cylinder against manufacturer's original specification. If any one cylinder shows much less compression than any of the others, component wear must be suspected, and a re-build may be in order.

Your inboard's transmission needs regular maintenance, especially its lubrication system. Check your transmission's oil level at recommended intervals; and make sure its coolant system (usually a portion of the raw-water circuit) is not leaking – either into the transmission itself, or into the bilge.

The engine in a small cruiser is usually bedded beneath the cockpit, directly abaft the companionway steps. The steps should come away completely to offer access to the engine's oil filter, fuel lines and fuel filter, cooling water intake (and its valve), cooling water strainer, and other maintenance items – all these should be close to hand.

Finally, the engine's compartment, when closed off from the rest of the boat should be as sound-proof as possible to keep the inevitable rumble to a relatively dull roar.

SOME POINTS TO CONSIDER IF YOUR DIESEL ENGINE FAILS

Should anything SEEM wrong – high temperature, rough running, frequent stoppages, oil pressure fluctuations – STOP THE ENGINE IMMEDIATELY! Failure to do so may cause major damage. Remember that anything that moves needs maintenance. As much as you might hate the 'iron jib', it is part of the boat and needs the same care as the brightwork and winches.

If the engine stops of its own accord, switch off the ignition. Check the fuel system. Filters must be free of dirt and water. They should be filled with oil. The possibility exists that the tanks are empty. The filters may be only partly filled if this is the case. However, partial filter filling may also be due to a fuel line blockage. If the engine won't restart, you will have to bleed both filters and possibly injectors. Consult your owner's manual.

Overheating is the most common problem with diesels and is most often due to a torn or failed water-cooling pump impeller. First, though, check the water inlet for debris and blockage. Also check the belt to the water pump. Make sure the propeller is not fouled. This is the place to warn you: ALWAYS CARRY A SPARE IMPELLER. Changing it is a 10-minute job at most, but for want of a spare, you may be disabled until you can signal for a tow or the breeze picks up.

Oil pressure dropping can indicate a major problem. Check the oil level and top up. If water has mixed with the oil, the head gasket may have ruptured. Do not run the engine above very low rpms (no higher than 1500 rpm in most modern marine diesels).

If the engine will not start, yet the starter motor is turning over, the glow plug may need replacement.

Uneven running may be due to a clogged or broken injector. If possible, replace; if not, run engine very slowly.

A full spare parts kit as well as the manufacturer's manual should be aboard for anything more than a day sail. Read the manual before setting out on a cruise. Make sure you have the necessary tools on board.

ENGINE FAILURE

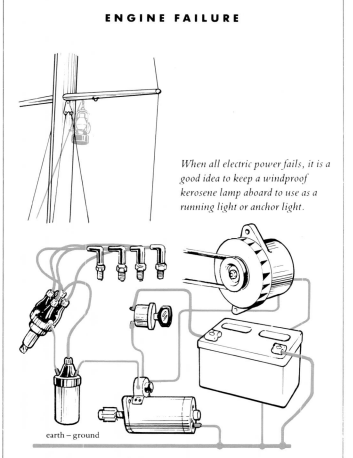

When all electric power fails, it is a good idea to keep a windproof kerosene lamp aboard to use as a running light or anchor light.

earth – ground

Basic knowledge of how a gasoline engine works is a must if your auxiliary is so equipped. The things to watch out for are dampness and poor contacts in the electrical connections.

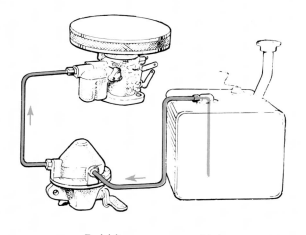

Fuel delivery systems are critical. The tank must be corrosion-free, the carburetor clean and the fuel pump running.

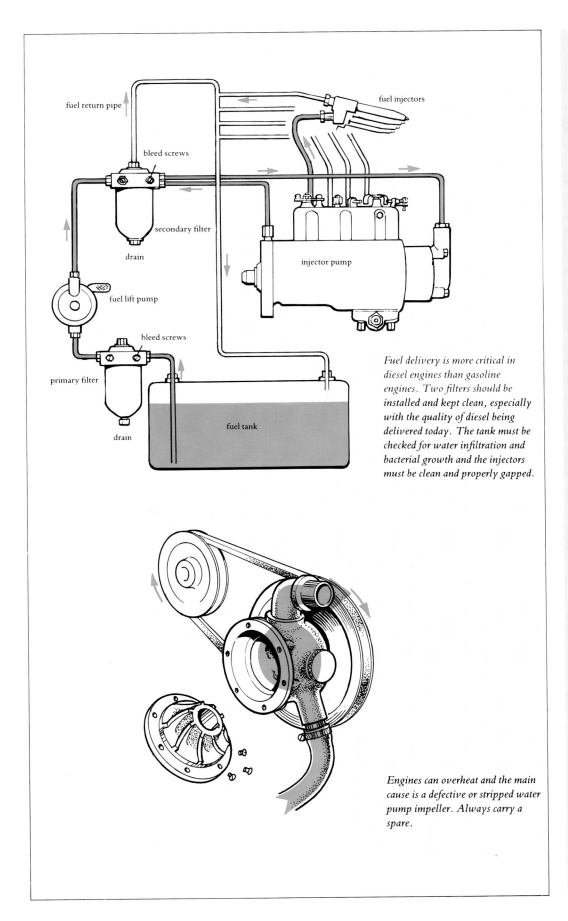

fuel return pipe

bleed screws

secondary filter

drain

fuel lift pump

bleed screws

primary filter

drain

fuel tank

fuel injectors

injector pump

Fuel delivery is more critical in diesel engines than gasoline engines. Two filters should be installed and kept clean, especially with the quality of diesel being delivered today. The tank must be checked for water infiltration and bacterial growth and the injectors must be clean and properly gapped.

Engines can overheat and the main cause is a defective or stripped water pump impeller. Always carry a spare.

SOME POINTS TO CONSIDER IF YOUR GASOLINE ENGINE FAILS

Check the electrical system. The battery may be dead, especially if the starter motor will not turn over. A connection between the battery ignition switch and starter motor circuit may be defective. Check the spark plugs and distributor head. Often, only the plugs will have to be replaced; always carry spares.

If the engine stops with grinding and clanking noises, serious damage is probably at hand. If no noise occurs, an electrical fault is probable and should be traced as above. If it hesitates and stops, the fault is most likely with the fuel system. Check as per instruction manual. The fuel tank may be empty. If not, there is probably a blockage in the line, or the fuel pump may have malfunctioned. Blow out the fuel line. If still no result, dismantle or replace the pump.

Overheating will be caused by a blocked water inlet, a broken pump, low oil level or a fouled propeller. In any case, if the temperature rises, turn off the engine immediately.

Drop in oil pressure. Stop engine and check oil level. Refill as necessary. Do not run engine unless absolutely necessary.

Uneven running is probably due to a fouled plug or bad timing. Replace plug. If unevenness persists, have a mechanic look at it.

TENDERS AND DINGHIES

A rigid tender with captive oarlocks, fenders, a pump, and sculling notch.

TENDERS: SUBSIDIARY DINGHIES

Few boats can do without a tender. Even if you have a marina berth or a mooring served by a club's launch service, there will always be the need to ferry the crew and stores to and from the shore.

The tender is also useful for working the boat, laying out a kedge anchor or taking lines away from the boat to another point. Children will find one an enjoyable diversion, rowing or sailing around an anchorage.

Few dinghies can serve all needs efficiently and most are a compromise.

The main distinction here is between rigid and inflatable tenders.

Rigid tenders have been with us for many years and a neat, wooden clinker dinghy hanging in davits is an ideal adjunct to proper cruising. Unfortunately, such dinghies are now very expensive, heavy and can only stow on larger yachts. The modern cruiser has such a large coachroof to give good headroom below that clear deck space is at a premium. If they cannot be carried on deck, then such dinghies must be towed.

If your boat lies at an exposed mooring a dinghy like this may be the best way to get out from the shore, especially if it is a good rowing dinghy. Rigid tenders are now also made in fiberglass and plywood, which helps to reduce their cost.

They will need good fendering to protect your topsides, and metal rub rails underneath to prevent damage when beaching. If you find the dinghy knocking against the boat, on the turn of the tide for instance, stream a bucket on a warp from the stern of the tender to help hold it clear.

Inflatable dinghies have the great advantage of being easy to stow. Deflated in their containers, they should fit most cockpit lockers, while half deflated they can be rolled up and stowed on deck. They are also very good load carriers and can be brought alongside without fear of damaging the topsides.

They have disadvantages too: firstly, despite being amazingly tough they can be punctured by jagged rocks or sharp projections. Secondly, their mobility and maneuverability are poor compared to those of a nicely-shaped rigid tender. They have little directional stability and inertia and they are subject to windage so that they crab around on the surface. In a sea, their high buoyancy makes them bob up and down, dissipating forward motion, necessitating the curious technique of using short, fast, light rowing strokes rather than the nice, long sweeps characteristic of rigid dinghy rowing.

Yet for all this, inflatables are the answer to many people's needs. Fixed wooden transoms give more shape to the floor and enhance rowing capability as well as making the use of a small outboard motor simple. Floorboards also enhance performance. There is a new generation of rigid-bottom inflatable which rows, sails, and powers surprisingly well, and can even be used as a liferaft when CO_2 inflation and canopy options are specified.

Too many mishaps occur on, what is for many, the shortest part of the cruise – the journey from shore out to the boat. Tenders are unstable due to their size, yet very often they are overloaded with crew not wearing personal flotation devices.

When the tender is launched from either the jetty or the boat, its painter or tow rope should be made fast, perhaps around a cleat, and led back to whoever is in the dinghy. Normally it is the oarsman who boards first, stepping smoothly into the middle of the dinghy. Other crew members go fore and aft so the tender is loaded evenly. Disembarking is a reverse of this process.

To get under way the outboard oar can be shipped, and when the crew push the tender clear, the inboard can also be shipped. Underway, consideration must be given to wind and tide. Rarely can you aim directly for your destination but rather some distance upwind or uptide from it. You will often see a rower stopping at the transom of the boat, only to have the tide carry the tender away from the craft before the crew has made contact.

When approaching the boat or dock you should aim more or less at the 'target'. With a boatlength to go, unship the inboard oar so that the blade and rowlocks cannot damage the topsides of the boat. Then with the remaining oar hold the blade in the water so that the tender pivots on it and turns around parallel to the boat or dock. Get it right, and you will be able to reach out and make the painter fast to finish a neat display of boat handling. More to the point, it prevents ramming the 'target' with the dinghy's bow and stops the crew having to reach ahead from the least stable part of the dinghy.

When towing a tender, make sure every loose item is removed or securely lashed down – oars, oarlocks, bailer, etc. A strong line should be used for the tow line and secured firmly. Modern, shiny, synthetic ropes can slip on a smooth cleat, especially with the intermittent tugging exerted by the tender. The dinghy attachment must also be strong, a through-bolt on a rigid tender and a strap on an inflatable one.

How long a line is a matter of experiment. In strong winds an inflatable might have to have a short line so that the bow is almost brought aboard the boat, otherwise it will spin crazily in the wind. A rigid tender will surf in a following sea and try and overtake the parent boat. A long line or a small drogue towed behind the dinghy will help to stop it from slewing around.

When you maneuver under power, shorten the tow rope right up, or bring the tender alongside to prevent it from fouling the propeller.

Tenders of course can be fun in safe conditions. A regatta tender race for women.

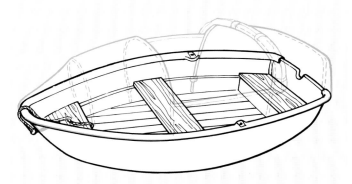

A dinghy can be turned into a liferaft with foresight and some work. Flotation, a canopy, stores and some means of propulsion must be added.

When boarding a dinghy from a dock or pier, always step into the center of the boat while holding on to the edge of the dock or a rail. Sit down squarely as soon as possible. Only then should you consider untying the painter.

THE SAILING DINGHY

The sailing dinghy is the raw material of which sailors are built. Almost all successful skippers serve their time in dinghies of various descriptions.

There are many reasons why the dinghy is such a valuable learning tool and they include the speed and accuracy with which it responds to steering input and weight shift; the simplicity of its rig; its durability; its portability; and its low cost.

Of all these, the first is by far the most important in the long run. Learn how to manage a small sailing dinghy in a strong breeze and a bit of a sea, and you'll be able to handle almost anything. Things happen fast in a dinghy; mistakes are proven immediately, yet at the same time are easily and quickly corrected given the proper curative action.

The hull of a modern sailing dinghy is usually built of several layers of fiberglass cloth laminated and encapsulated in hardened resin. A fiberglass boat like this is usually built using a mold, in which the hull is allowed to cure before it is removed and fitted with its other components.

The boat's length is simply that – length – but is measured in two places, and designated LWL, or length at the waterline, and LOA, or length overall.

The typical sailing dinghy hull will have a LOA of roughly 8–10ft (2.5–3m); a LWL of about 6–9ft (1.8–2.7m); a beam of about 3½–5ft (1–1.5m); a draft of perhaps 5in (13cm) with the centerboard all the way up, and about 3 feet with the board down; and a freeboard of 1–2ft (30–60cm). A dinghy might weigh a mere 75lb (34kg) without any of its gear aboard, or several hundred with everything aboard.

As we've seen, the centerboard acts to provide lateral resistance as the wind tries to push the boat sideways under a press of sail. But the best thing about a centerboard, especially when it is applied to a sailing dinghy, is that it carries little or no weight (it is *unballasted*), it stores easily, and it can be raised for shallow water operations.

The dinghy rudder is normally detachable and is mounted on pairs of hinge mechanisms that can be uncoupled. These *gudgeons* (the 'female' part of the hinge) and *pintles* (the male part) are stainless steel or bronze components. The gudgeons are mounted one above the other at the aftermost part of the hull (called the *transom*). The pintles are mounted on the rudder itself in corresponding fashion, so that the pairs mate when fitted together.

Round bilge hull shapes are often, but not always, used for high performance racing dinghies. The simpler hard-chine designs are ideal for amateur boat-building. Round bilge (1). Hard-chine (2).

SOME POINTS TO CONSIDER ABOUT YOUR DINGHY

More deaths are probably caused by swamped and capsized dinghies than by anything else on the water. The average tender is perhaps 8 or 10 feet (2.5 or 3m) in length and cannot really hold more than three people in anything but a dead calm. In truly rough water, no more than two should attempt a journey. As well as not overloading with people, you must be careful to avoid masses of gear, especially in the ends of the boat. Try to keep the boat trimmed and balanced, athwartships and fore-and-aft.

The novice will inevitably step on the gunwale when trying to board. This can lead to lacerations or a dunking. In most hard tenders, you can step directly into the center portion of the floorboards. However, if the dock or float is particularly high, you may have to step on the center thwart and descend quickly. The idea is to sit down as quickly as possible. NEVER board a dinghy with your hands full. Either load first or enter and then transfer the cargo once you are seated.

Probably the greatest danger – other than overloading – is in landing or launching through surf. If the surf is running with any power, you would be well advised to stay on the ship or on the beach. Otherwise you'll need a large enough boat to power through. Do not underestimate the power of breaking seas.

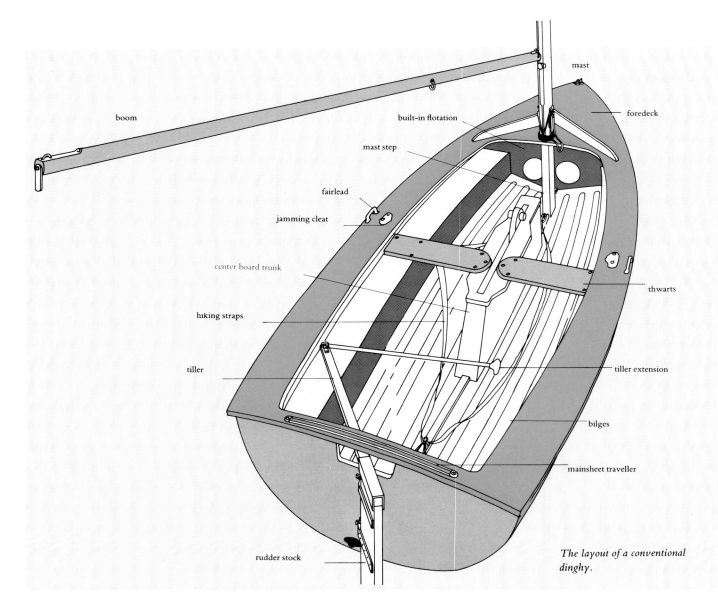

boom

mast

built-in flotation

foredeck

mast step

fairlead

jamming cleat

center board trunk

thwarts

hiking straps

tiller

tiller extension

bilges

mainsheet traveller

rudder stock

The layout of a conventional dinghy.

A dinghy may or may not have seats for its crew. Most multi purpose dinghies have *thwarts*, or transverse seats. Thwarts are usually suspended from the outer edges of the boat's hull, the *gunwales*. The center thwart is the one on which the oarsman sits when rowing the dinghy, and is usually attached to the centerboard trunk as an added stiffening member. On some dinghies, that's all there will be; others may have forward and after thwarts as well.

Seats or thwarts will often carry enclosed flotation material, and boats with wide side-decks will often have their flotation built-in under the deck area.

At or near the dinghy's transom, there should be a self-bailing device. Normally a small 'trap-door' built into the boat's bottom near the stern, this device is designed to be opened when the boat becomes uncomfortably full of water. The motion of the boat is usually enough to suck out the water from inside.

The mast is the principal *spar* of any sailing boat. On

some dinghies, the mast can be broken down into two parts for stowage purposes. Most performance dinghies, however, have one-piece masts.

There are two types of *rigging*: *standing rigging* and *running rigging*. Small dinghies do not usually need standing rigging, as mast loads are minimal due to the small sail area and relatively high strength of the materials used in the rig. However, a larger boat with tall mast and much more sail, needs stays and shrouds to help support its rig. The size of boat where standing rigging becomes important is about 13–14ft (3.9–4.2m).

Running rigging provides sail control. It is composed of lines and cordage that attach to points on the boat's sail or sails and are hauled or slacked to manipulate them against the wind.

Most sailing dinghies only need one sail – the mainsail. However, some have a small sail forward of the mast, called the *jib*. A dinghy with a jib is said to be 'sloop-rigged', while a single-sailed boat is a 'catboat'.

I N D E X

*Numbers in italic refer to
illustrations*

I N D E X